THE FIRE OF GOD'S LOVE

Sequel to The Fire of Delayed Answers

BOB SORGE

To Marci, my beloved wife and best friend:

Sweetheart, you've stood at my side these past four years. We've walked together, wept together, waited together, and worshiped together. I always knew you were God's gift to me, but it's been during our season of fire that I've come to appreciate you more than words could ever express. Instead of separating us, the pressure has bonded us more tightly than ever. Above all, I am so grateful for our shared passion that the fire has inflamed — an abandoned delight in the face of our Lord Jesus Christ.

CONTENTS

SECTION SIX: THE GREATEST IS LOVE

Section One

FURNACE
OF
LOVE

1

GOD'S FIERY LOVE

The most sublime theme in all of Scripture is the love of God. There is nothing higher or nobler toward which we can direct our meditation. God's love is altogether wonderful, beyond our complete comprehension, and entirely inexhaustible in its scope and intensity.

To know and experience the love of Christ is the happy and eternal pursuit of all God's saints. It is an ocean that beckons our exploration, a massive sun that blazes like the face of God Himself. Its gravitational force derives from its sheer immensity, pulling the awe-struck believer into the heart of its blazing inferno.

River Of Love

Love is the thing that moves and mobilizes God. It is the energy source which empowers all of His activity toward us. Should you tap into God's divine power source, you will discover that it is a rush-flow of electric love that will drive and carry you along as well.

There is a river that flows from the throne of God; the Bible calls it "the river of life." But I am suggesting that its current is "love." The outflow of God's life is propelled toward us by His love.

I do not envision this river coming to us as a serpentine, meandering, lazy river that barely ambles along as it shuffles toward mankind. No, it is a swift-flowing, sweep-you-off-your-feet kind of torrential current. Like the churning waters of a flood-stage river, the love of God is unstoppable. It is violent, overwhelming, ruinous—it is **destructive**.

"Destructive?" someone might ask. "How is God's love destructive?" To be straightforward, it was the love of God that took Jesus to His death. It is this love which has inextricably captured the hearts of the martyrs over the centuries. When the love of God pulls you into its vortex, it will very possibly lead you to your death, too.

Ah, blessed death! which produces everlasting life.

Swept Away

Paul tells us that he was "compelled" by this love. "For the love of Christ compels us," he writes in Second Corinthians 5:14. This New Testament word "compel" means literally "to hold together" or "to grip tightly."

It is the word that is used at Jesus' arrest to describe the manner in which they "held" Him (Luke 22:63). So in using this word "compels," Paul is basically saying, "I got arrested, bound, and incarcerated by this love."

I can hear Paul testifying, "I decided to make the love of God my singular pursuit. But when I found it, His love grabbed hold of me, swept me off my feet, caught me up in its vice-grip, and now my life is completely out of my control. I am being propelled forward by a force greater than my ability to resist. I have no choice; this love is squeezing the very life out of me."

Paul is saying, "I am in a headlock. I have been captured—I am a slave to a love that is beyond my imagination. The love of God has taken hold of me, and I am no longer my own."

Be warned: **step out into the river of God's love, and your life will career out of control too**. If you surrender yourself to the current of God's love, you too will lose all control to a love that may take you, as it did Peter, a way in which you don't want to go (see John 21:18).

The Unity Within The Godhead

We understand from the Scriptures that the Godhead is comprised of three distinct Persons—Father, Son, and Holy Spirit—who abide in such incredible unity of heart and purpose and understanding that they are said to be One. Their oneness is so complete that we do not have three Gods, but one God. This is the mystery of the Trinity.

What force would be so great that it would take three eternally self-existent Persons and meld them together into such a cohesive unity that they call themselves One?

The fusion of three distinct personalities into one Godhead would require a force greater than the gravity of the largest stars. It would require a gravity greater than that of what astronomers call a "black hole," the gravity of which is thought to be so powerful that even light rays are not able to escape it, and thus it appears as a formless hole in the expanses of space.

What strength of gravity would have such an inward pull that it would not even allow light to escape its clutches? And yet the even more profound question is, what sort of gravity would fuse the three Persons of the Godhead into One?

This force that unites the Godhead—greater than the gravitational pull of the most powerfully imploding stars—is none other than love. **Love is the thing that binds the Trinity together**.

Jesus pointed to this love that exists within the Godhead when He said, "I in them, and You in Me; that they may be made perfect in one, and that the world may know that You have sent Me, *and have loved them as You have loved Me*" (John 17:23).

Imagine it: the Father's heart is drawn toward you in the same intensity of passion with which He loves the Son! It is an immeasurably awesome gravity that has pulled the Son into the heart of the Father, the Spirit unto the Son, and the Father unto the Spirit. This love that joins the Trinity together is beyond all human comprehension. It is eternal in its intensity, its longevity, and its dimensions.

And here's the incredible part. This immeasurable force, this flaming love, reserved in its exclusivity throughout eternity to just three Persons, has now chosen to reach out and pull in a fourth—you!

Even as Nebuchadnezzar looked into a flaming furnace centuries ago and saw the form of a fourth person in the fire (Daniel 3:25), so too there is a flaming furnace of eternal love into which the angels now look, *and they see the form of a fourth*! There is a dimension of love that for all eternity had been reserved to just three, and now the cherubim and living creatures gaze with rapt wonder as they behold the form of a fourth in that eternal furnace of divine love. And this fourth has to them the form and appearance of the Bride of Christ.

Face To Face

Words and music:
Bob Sorge

Section Two

THE
CROSS

2

THREE DIMENSIONS OF GOD'S LOVE

The Bride of Christ has gained access to the love that blazes within the Godhead through the cross of Jesus Christ.

Not long ago, as I was reading the accounts of Christ's passion in the Gospels, I began to pray, "Lord, show me Your cross." I had a great sense of having but a limited understanding of all that Christ accomplished in His crucifixion, and a deep desire for the meaning of the cross to become my personal possession.

As I prayed in this way, I began to see that the entire point of the cross and suffering of Jesus is, in a word, love. **The purpose of the cross is to demonstrate and incite love**. It is the ultimate demonstration of God's love, and it is the primary incentive God uses to awaken love in the hearts of sincere believers.

The cross displays three wondrous dimensions of God's love, and the first one I want to point to is this: the love of Christ for us.

Christ's Love For Us

When we behold the cross, we are impacted with how much Christ Jesus must love us! Truly He is like the merchant in the parable who sacrificed everything in order to purchase one pearl of great price (Matthew 13:45-46). To Christ, the redemption of His Bride is of supreme value and was worth the sacrifice of Calvary.

The Scriptures point to Christ's great love for us:

- Now before the feast of the Passover, when Jesus knew that His hour had come that He should depart from this world to the Father, having loved His own who were in the world, He loved them to the end (John 13:1).
- Who shall separate us from the love of Christ? (Romans 8:35).
- For the love of Christ compels us (2 Corinthians 5:14).
- To know the love of Christ which passes knowledge; that you may be filled with all the fullness of God (Ephesians 3:19).
- To Him who loved us and washed us from our sins in His own blood (Revelation 1:5).

Christ's great love for mankind is seen on the cross during His two brief conversations with others:
1) To the dying thief on the cross: "Jesus said to him, 'Assuredly, I say to you, today you will be with Me in Paradise'" (Luke 23:43).
2) To His disciple John and His mother: "When Jesus therefore saw His mother, and the disciple whom He loved standing by, He said to His mother, 'Woman, behold your son!' Then He said to the disciple, 'Behold your mother!' And from that hour that disciple took her to his own home" (John 19:26-27).

Jesus could have thought to Himself, "I don't have energy to pay attention to these people. I'm in too much pain, I've got to concentrate entirely on enduring to the end. I'm saving the whole world right now, and I can't be distracted with one or two people who happen to be here at this moment."

Instead, Jesus reached out to His fellow man despite His own personal anguish. His great love extended past the horrendous pain of Calvary and touched those who looked to Him.

Christ's example of reaching out in the midst of great personal pain continues to be a great model for all believers. Even when we're hurting ourselves, the love of Christ wants to burst forth from our hearts to the needy who surround us.

The cross is the graphic emblem of Christ's love for us, and yet when we take a closer look, we see that it points even more vividly to yet another dimension of Christ's love. The love of Jesus for mankind is not the most gripping love that the cross displays. Many have enjoyed the words to the popular Christian song, "When He was on the cross, I was on His mind," and yet I'm not convinced that's true.

While suffering on the cross, Jesus wasn't thinking primarily about us. The evidence suggests that He was thinking primarily about His Father. This is the second great love that the cross displays: Jesus' love for the Father.

Jesus' Love For The Father

The mutual passion that exists within the Godhead is so intense that Jesus was willing to pay any price in order to fulfill the request of His Father. The death of the cross was the Father's will, and so Jesus offered to His Father these great words of love before His arrest: "Nevertheless, not as I will, but as You will" (Matthew 26:39). Jesus was basically saying, "I love You so much, My Father, I'll do **anything** for You!"

In Gethsemane, Jesus established with finality His willingness to go to Calvary because of His passion for the Father. Gethsemane had nothing to do with the devil.

The devil had long since given up trying to entice Jesus; all he could do now was try to kill Him. Gethsemane had nothing to do with overcoming temptation; it had to do with the love of the Lamb for the Father as He embraced the Father's will. Gethsemane was an exchange of love at its deepest levels.

To endure the horror of God's wrath, Jesus had to have a high degree of mental **focus** while impaled to the cross. To the end, His focus was upon one Person, the Father. This is seen in the three statements He directed exclusively to His Father during His crucifixion:

- "Father, forgive them, for they do not know what they do" (Luke 23:34).

- "My God, My God, why have you forsaken Me?" (Matthew 27:46).

- "Father, into Your hands I commit My spirit" (Luke 23:46).

It is almost inconceivable that, in the face of the pain Jesus suffered on the cross, and the fact that He had the power at His immediate disposal to be released from the cross in an instant, He chose to stay on the cross in incomprehensible agony. There can be only one reason for such focus, for such toleration of suffering. Jesus was willing to endure the pain of Calvary because there was something to be gained that was greater than the pain. "Who for the joy that was set before Him endured the cross" (Hebrews 12:2). What joyful thing did He look forward to which enabled Him to endure the cross? Someone might suggest, "It was a Bride! Jesus was looking forward to the joy of redeeming a wife to Himself."

That answer is partly true, but it's not the primary joy that was set before the Lord. **Above all else, Jesus looked ahead to the joy of receiving His Father's affirmation—the explosive, extravagant delight the Father would abundantly lavish upon Him in glory**. The greatest joy He could know would be to hear His Father say, "Well done, My Son, I am well pleased with You! You have done My will."

The joy of His Father's approving embrace was, for our Lord Jesus, worth all the pain of the cross.

Jesus had the power to come off His cross, and we too have the power to come down off our own cross. What is it that will keep us impaled to the crucified life? Nothing short of overflowing love for the Son of God, and a passion for the love which He is capable of bestowing. If we truly value the honor that comes from God, we will chase after the crucified life; it is the pathway to receiving His delight.

In His heart Jesus was saying, "Father, I love You so much that if going to the cross pleases Your heart, I'll do it. I'll do **anything** to please You!" Thus, the cross is a passionate display of the Son's love for the Father. **The cross cries out, "Anything for love!"**

The Father's Love For The World

The third great love that the cross displays is the love of the Father for the world. "For God so loved the world that He gave His only begotten Son, that whoever believes in Him should not perish but have everlasting life" (John 3:16).

If you want to know what God's love for you is like, behold the cross. The cross is the Father's way of saying to the world, "This is how much I love you!"

It is easy for us to suppose that God must hate the world. But to the contrary, He has great passion for the world. It's true that God hates the world system, but He desperately loves the people of the world.

The intensity of God's love for the world is better appreciated when we consider God's vehement love for His Son. "This is My beloved Son in whom I am well pleased!" To use human terminology, the Father is head-over-heels **crazy** over His Son! To God, His Son is in a league all His own. The Father has many mighty and holy attendants in His heavenly courts, but none enjoys the status and privilege of the Son. He ranks above the entire created order and is the recipient of the Father's most exclusive and eternal affections.

There has never been nor ever will be a force greater than the love which draws the heart of the Father into the heart of the Son. So in the light of the Father's fiery love for His Son, we must ask the question, "What would cause the Father, who loves His only begotten Son so intensely, to crucify His Son and then pour the full punishment for mankind's sin upon Him?"

It seems incredulous—almost preposterous That God would turn on His Son, the object of His most intimate affections, and consign Him to a vicious and torturous death? Unthinkable! And yet—it happened!

"Why?" the angels ask.

"For what reason is the Father doing this to His only begotten?" the heavenly hosts ask of each other.

The astounding answer is found in these simple words, "For God so loved the world." **He loved you and me so much that He nailed His precious Son to a tree, beaten and scourged, and then lacerated Him with His own infinite wrath against sin.** The implications of suffering the Father's wrath against sin are so horrific that no one but God Himself could bear such agony. No one

has suffered, dear friends, as much as God has. All this pain—
because He loves **you** so very much!

The cross was the best way the Father knew to express to the
world how much He loves us.

To endure the suffering of His Son, and to pour out His wrath
upon Him until the vial was empty, the Father had to have **focus**.
What was the thing upon which the Father focussed that enabled
Him to endure throughout the suffering of His Son? The Father's
focus was on **us**. Through every excruciating moment the Father
kept reminding Himself, "We must pay the full price for their redemption—because I love them so much." The Father's focus,
during Calvary's horror, was on us.

God gave us a picture of what this was like for Him when He
asked Abraham to kill his only son, Isaac. We're able to imagine
what it must have been like for Abraham to lift a knife above his
son's body—the only son his wife Sarah had borne to him in their
old age. A knife was cutting through his own soul as he prepared
to plunge the blade through Isaac's heart. God asked Abraham to
do this so that we might hear the Father's heartbeat, "This image
gives you a glimpse into what it was like for Me to kill My only
begotten Son."

Such pain is endured only when there is something to be gained
that is greater than the pain. What, in the eyes of the Father, was to
be gained that was worth such pain? It was the Bride that He would
present to His Son.

I can imagine the Father thinking, "Son, hang in there. Hold
on just a little longer. Drink the cup all the way to the bottom
because it will be worth it! I'm telling You, Son, I'm preparing a
Bride for you. She will be so beautiful, and O, You will love her so
much! She will understand You, You'll be able to relate to her, she
will be a co-equal partner with You, she'll be compatible with you
in every way, and she will be like You. What's more, she will love
You with the same love with which I love You. Oh yes, My Son,
this Bride will enrapture Your heart. She will be worth these few
brief hours of pain. You must persevere to the death."

The Father could endure Calvary because He saw a Bride for
His Son. You see, the Father is so crazy about His Son that He is in

the business of preparing as much glory as He possibly can for His Son. He is ardently committed to garnering lavish affection for the Son of His love. During His Son's suffering, the Father saw the love that would be cultivated within the heart of the Bride for His Son.

That's all the Father wants—to see love poured on His Son. **This is the Father's creative search, to find increasingly glorious ways for the Son to receive the love and adoration that is due Him.** The Father looked ahead and said, "Son, believe Me, it will be worth it. Not only will she move Your heart with her beauty, but O, she will love You! She will love you with an eternal love! Trust Me, Son—it will be worth it!"

The cross extravagantly cries, "**Anything** for love."

The great issue for mankind is this: "Will you love Him?" It's not simply, "Will you believe Him?" because even the demons believe and tremble. The haunting question of all time continues to be the one that Jesus posed to Simon Peter after Peter had denied Him. Jesus asked Peter, "Do you love Me?" This is the great soul-searching question that each one of us must answer.

Jesus didn't die so that people would dissect and analyze the benefits of the gospel, and then based on their assessment of the data make a rational choice to believe that Jesus is the Son of God. No, He died for much more than that. He died for your **love**. He will never be satisfied with anything less than your freewill, non-coerced, voluntary affections and desires.

3

THE CROSS: INVITATION TO LOVE

The Pinnacle Passion

We tend to rate the significance of an event or thing according to the level of emotion we felt at the time. The highest points in our lives have been those times of greatest pleasure or deepest joy; the lowest times have been those moments of greatest heartache, grief, and pain. We always remember the highest highs and the lowest lows. Extremely emotional events will always remain etched in our memories.

In the same way, there is one event in the history of all eternity that will forever stand out to God as the most significant event for Him. That one event is the crucifixion. **There is nothing — not even eternity itself — that will ever erase from God's mind the slightest fraction of the vivid reality of Calvary's horror**. We have no idea how the Father's heart wept and heaved over His Son, as Christ bore the wrath of sin. It is the deepest pain God has ever or ever will know.

God is as passionate today about the cross as He was during the six hours of Christ's impalement. When it comes to the cross, God is anything but stoic or unaffected. Every remembrance of the cross stirs up infinite zeal and passion within His breast. The cross is the ultimate expression of how powerful God's emotions toward us really are.

God doesn't relate to impassive Christians. He identifies with Christians whose hearts move and stir and cry within them. There is nothing in the way the Triune God has ever related to mankind that is stoic or impassive or unaffected or staid. The cross demands an extravagant and abandoned response of grateful affection from the people of God. God is interested in nothing less.

The Ultimate Expression Of Love

If you want to be awakened in your fervency for Jesus, look at the cross. As you gaze upon the cross, where God's love is so graphically displayed, you will be awakened to a fuller, deeper bridal love. As you behold His passion and suffering, you will get swept up in the current of His fiery love.

The cross was God's best way of saying, "I love you." Without words, the cross speaks the language of love. It renders love a vocabulary — it's the ultimate expression of love.

The cross is the most articulate and passionate way to say, "I love you." This is the reason why Jesus invites us to take up our cross. By calling us to take up our cross, Jesus is inviting us to love Him with everything within us. He is saying, "I invite you to love Me in the same way that I love you. I am giving you the opportunity to return to Me the kind of love I am pouring upon you."

Thus, the cross is an invitation to love. To take up my cross is to enter into a reciprocating love relationship with Jesus of awesome proportions. When I take up my cross, I am qualifying for a depth of love relationship that is unparalleled with any love relationship I've ever imagined. I am opening myself to God's dimension of love, and the cross is the best way to express this kind of fiery God-love.

When Jesus says, "Take up your cross and follow Me," sometimes we imagine such a lifestyle as the most morbid and boring existence a human being might possibly entertain. But quite to the contrary, when we take up our cross at Christ's command we find ourselves catapulted into a dimension of love that is altogether sublime, more wonderful than any earthly love we've ever experienced, and so fulfilling that for the first time in our lives we feel like we're really starting to live.

The call to the cross is not something to be dreaded and avoided, but it is an invitation to the most exciting and fulfilling existence that man can possibly enjoy. You will lose everything—and you'll gain everything!

Christ's Incredible Offer

On one occasion, Jesus was approached by a young aristocratic Jew who felt like he was missing something in his spiritual life. This devout young man had adhered to the commandments all his life, and was wondering what else he needed to do to inherit eternal life. Let's look at the story:

> Now as He was going out on the road, one came running, knelt before Him, and asked Him, "Good Teacher, what shall I do that I may inherit eternal life?" So Jesus said to him, "Why do you call Me good? No one is good but One, that is, God. You know the commandments: 'Do not commit adultery,' 'Do not murder,' 'Do not steal,' 'Do not bear false witness,' 'Do not defraud,' 'Honor your father and your mother.'" And he answered and said to Him, "Teacher, all these things I have kept from my youth." Then Jesus, looking at him, loved him, and said to him, "One thing you lack: Go your way, sell whatever you have and give to the poor, and you will have treasure in heaven; and come, take up the cross, and follow Me." But he was sad at this word, and went away sorrowful, for he had great possessions (Mark 10:17-22).

The writer tells us, "Then Jesus, looking at him, loved him." What Jesus is about to say are words spoken from a heart of genuine love for this young man. And what are these words of eternal love? "Sell whatever you have and give to the poor, and you will have treasure in heaven; and come, take up the cross, and follow Me." (v.21)

"What?" our human nature wants to respond. "You call that love? How can it be a loving thing to ask someone to sell all his possessions?"

When we read Christ's calls to discipleship and taking up the cross, we tend to hear a tone of voice that is almost mean-spirited. "If I have to die," we imagine Jesus grousing, "then you have to die too." But this caricature is far from the heart of Christ's call to this rich young ruler.

What we sometimes fail to realize is that His call to the cross is an appeal of love. More than that, it is an appeal **to** love. It is an invitation to a love relationship. "If you are willing to put away all your other loves," Jesus is actually telling this young man with many possessions, "you will enter into the delight of a love relationship with Me." Jesus loved this man so much that He actually unveiled to Him the glorious secret of an extravagant love relationship with the altogether Lovely One—the Son of God. **Every call of Christ to self-denial and discipleship is in fact an invitation to a depth of love relationship that exceeds all our expectations or dreams.**

This young man went away sorrowful, thinking that Jesus had offered him a lousy deal. When you understand what Jesus was actually offering this fellow, it's almost unbelievable to conceive that he would turn it down. To illustrate, suppose a homeless man living in the slums of Mexico City happens to win the New York Lottery. In order to receive the $10 million he has just won, however, he is told that he must relocate to the United States. "What?" the fellow cries. "I've got to leave my hometown? You're telling me I have to leave my neighborhood I know, and all my friends? I grew up here; my family is all here; everything I know is right here. The sacrifice seems so great, how can I do it?"

So the fellow turns down the $10 million because he thinks they're trying to deprive him of something. That's what the rich young ruler did with Jesus. He thought Jesus was trying to deprive him of something, when in actuality, Jesus was making him an incredible offer of love.

Jesus calls us to cast aside all worldly interests and to take up our cross and follow Him because in His infinite love He knows the benefits that await those who do so. You've got to see it as a love appeal. To accept His call to the cross is to embark upon an eternal love adventure with the God of the universe.

An Equally Fervent Exchange

There is nothing Christ wants more than a Bride who will love Him with the same kind of fiery zeal with which He loves her.

The letter to the church of Laodicea in Revelation 3 is one of the most terrifying passages in the entire Bible. Look again at what Jesus said to these believers:

> "I know your works, that you are neither cold nor hot. I could wish you were cold or hot. So then, because you are lukewarm, and neither cold nor hot, I will vomit you out of My mouth" (Revelation 3:15-16).

In my human understanding I want to respond, "Never, Lord! Surely You shall not do such a thing!" My natural mind is appalled that Christ would so peremptorily consign a believer to such a fate, simply because he was half-hearted in his commitment.

But then I look at the cross. And I see there a love that is ablaze with such a flaming fire that even death can't extinguish it. **O the fiery depths of this love that hangs there, mutilated and bleeding, and suffers willfully in order to win my love!**

Now, shall I look at that burning love on the cross, and lazily turn away to find another object with which to share my affections? After seeing the intensity of His love for me, shall I reciprocate with a milquetoast, insipid, inane, sleepy token of the leftovers of my love? Would that kind of fiery love want to receive a half-hearted, yawn-in-your-face love in return?

"NO!" declares He whose eyes are ablaze with an inflamed jealousy. "That kind of love is obnoxious to Me," He says. "I will vomit it out of My mouth."

Getting To Know Christ

If you really want to get to know Jesus, you need to gain a preoccupation with His cross. The cross is the only way to really get to know Him. This is what Paul pointed to:

> That I may know Him and the power of His resurrection,
> and the fellowship of His sufferings, being conformed to
> His death (Philippians 3:10).

We all want to get to know Jesus better, but we want to do so in a pathway that doesn't include suffering and death. Such a pathway simply doesn't exist. There's only one way to get to know Jesus, and that is through the cross.

We prefer to behold Jesus as He feeds the five thousand, or as He heals the sick, or as He walks on the water, or as He raises Lazarus from the dead. We find those images much more savory than the cross. But the cross is the wisdom and power of God, for it captures and portrays the essence of our beloved Lord.

"Then He said to them all, 'If anyone desires to come after Me, let him deny himself, and take up his cross daily, and follow Me'" (Luke 9:23). If you want to know Jesus, you've got to embrace the cross and "go after Him." This is not a leisurely keeping of pace behind Jesus, but it is an all-consuming, driving pursuit to catch up with Jesus. **Jesus reveals Himself to the one who takes up his cross and chases after Him.**

You won't get to know Christ by doing a research project in a theological library. You won't get to know Christ by meditating in isolation. You'll get to know the crucified Christ by sharing in His suffering. You must take up your cross and be crucified with Him in order to know Him as the crucified Christ. This is the motivation of taking up one's cross: "I want to know Him!"

4

EMBRACING DEATH

The Offence Of The Cross

A very noticeable shift took place at one point in Jesus' earthly ministry. This shift took place at the height of His popularity with the masses. Multiplied thousands thronged Him wherever He went, and everybody thought He was wonderful. Peter had just confessed to Him, "You are the Christ!" Jesus owns the appellation, and the disciples are beginning to realize what place in history they have come to inherit. It's at this moment of energy and excitement and momentum that Jesus immediately changes gears, and the thrust of His ministry takes on a dramatic change. The following passage records this shift:

> From that time Jesus began to show to His disciples that He must go to Jerusalem, and suffer many things from the elders and chief priests and scribes, and be killed, and be raised the third day. Then Peter took Him aside and began to rebuke Him, saying, "Far be it from You, Lord; this shall not happen to You!" But He turned and said to Peter, "Get behind Me, Satan! You are an offense to Me, for you are not mindful of the things of God, but the things of men" (Matthew 16:21-23).

Up to this point, Jesus hadn't whispered a hint about suffering, or being killed, or the cross. From this point on, He returns to this theme again and again. It was as Jesus shifted gears and began to talk about the cross that His popularity immediately began to diminish dramatically.

The disciples couldn't understand this kind of "cross talk." It made no sense to them, in the light of Jesus' burgeoning popularity, for Him to talk about being killed in Jerusalem. According to their script, that's not how the story was supposed to be written.

Peter was so disturbed by Jesus' "cross talk" that He immediately began to rebuke Jesus. "Don't talk like that, Lord—nothing like that is going to happen to You!"

Jesus responded by saying, "You offend Me." He was basically saying, "To suggest anything but suffering offends Me." We, in contrast, are all too easily offended at the suggestion that we might have to suffer. It's because we still haven't awakened to the relational possibilities with Christ that open to those who suffer with Him.

The Wisdom Of The Cross

The wisdom of the cross lies, in part, in this truth: there is no sufferer who cannot identify with the cross. No matter how excruciating the pain, every sufferer can lift his eyes to the cross of Christ and find comfort.

You can take the gospel to the gulag prisons of Siberia; you can take the gospel to the refugees of Africa; you can take the gospel to the street children of Brazil. There is no one who can curl up their lip and say they've suffered more than Jesus Christ. The cross extends hope to the most lonely sufferer.

And the cross transcends all age barriers. There is no child mature enough to speak who is incapable of understanding the cross. From the youngest age, children grasp the stark horror of the cross and understand how much Jesus must love them.

One of the chief purposes of suffering is to point us to the cross. When you're suffering, it's almost an instinctive response to look at the cross of Christ for comfort and consolation. Suffering is redeemed when we allow it to fix our gaze upon the cross.

The Anointing Of Death

It is as we embrace the death of the cross that the anointing is released in our lives. We do not choose the time or the way in which the cross comes before us. Such a death — death to self, goals, ambitions, desires, the praise of men, pleasures, worldly distractions, creature comforts — can be embraced only by the sovereign drawing of the Lord to that higher plane. We cannot just decide to die, for we are too full of ourselves. The Holy Spirit puts the cry in our hearts for more of the cross, and then He graciously answers that prayer.

Be ready, there's nothing more painful than death. And there's nothing more glorious than the life He can bring out of death. "Let this mind be in you which was also in Christ Jesus, who...became obedient to the point of death, even the death of the cross" (Philippians 2:5,8).

> Then Mary took a pound of very costly oil of spikenard, anointed the feet of Jesus, and wiped His feet with her hair. And the house was filled with the fragrance of the oil. Then one of His disciples, Judas Iscariot, Simon's son, who would betray Him, said, "Why was this fragrant oil not sold for three hundred denarii and given to the poor?" This he said, not that he cared for the poor, but because he was a thief, and had the money box; and he used to take what was put in it. But Jesus said, "Let her alone; she has kept this for the day of My burial" (John 12:3-7).

This story illustrates how the embracing of the cross releases a greater anointing in our lives. It says that Mary "anointed" Jesus for the day of His burial. Jesus was anointed to die. This fragrant oil represents the anointing of the Holy Spirit. The point is, when we fully embrace the cross and share in Christ's death, the anointing of the Holy Spirit comes upon us as well.

Where death is at work, there comes a greater release of the anointing. It's when we're full of ourselves (our own life) that we constrict the anointing, and so have to beg harder. When death is not at work in us, we try to get the anointing by praying harder.

If you're dead to self you're safe — God can entrust an anointing to you.

Paul came to realize that the apostolic call was a call to a greater death. He said, "Death is at work in us, but life is at work in you." The higher the calling, the greater the death.

Sometimes we tend to think of the cross as something horrible to bear, but what must be seen instead is the incredible flow of life and anointing that pours through the one who identifies with Christ's death.

The Church At Corinth

When Paul wrote about death being at work in him, most of his comments in that regard were written to the church at Corinth. To understand the implications of why Paul wrote about death to the Corinthians, we need to take a look at the particular challenges the Corinthians faced in their ministry.

Among all the New Testament churches, the church at Corinth is unique in that it enjoyed the greatest amount of freedom from persecution, oppression, suffering, and distress. Their challenges had much more to do with that of facing a hedonistic society. Corinth was imbued with a libertarian spirit. That's the mindset that says, "It's your thing, do what you want to do." The people of Corinth were fun-loving, pleasure-seeking, and gave each other a lot of space to pursue whatever turned them on. Thus, there was a great deal of toleration toward the Christians in Corinth.

In this atmosphere of freedom, the Corinthian church grew quickly. Their worship services were quite powerful. If you were to visit the church at Corinth for a congregational meeting, here are some dynamics you would have expected to experience:

1. You would notice they were strong believers (1 Corinthians 4:10).
2. You would witness the prolific exercise of spiritual gifts (1 Corinthians 1:7), which would include the evidence of prophecy, healings, and miracles.
3. You would enjoy great teaching (1 Corinthians 1:12). They had a flow of such outstanding teachers through

that church that they even had arguments over who was
the best teacher. They were well-fed and full (1
Corinthians 4:8).

4. You would notice that the believers were enjoying great
    prosperity (1 Corinthians 4:8). (Too bad Paul refused
    to receive a single offering while there; he could have
    made out pretty good.)
5. They were very tolerant and merciful to where people
    were at (1 Corinthians 5:1-2). They made everyone feel
    welcome and comfortable — to the point of even toler-
    ating teachers of a different gospel (2 Corinthians 11:4).
6. The church was theologically sound and orthodox in
    practice and tradition (1 Corinthians 11:2).
7. You would witness great liberty for personal expression
    (1 Corinthians 11:21; 14:26).
8. The atmosphere of their gatherings was electric with an
    air of vitality and a real sense of life (1 Corinthians 4:12).
9. They were very zealous (2 Corinthians 7:11; 9:2).
10. You would find corporate worship to be a high priority.
    At their request, Paul addressed more dynamics of cor-
    porate worship to this church than to any other church
    he wrote.

My point is this: Of all the New Testament churches, the church
at Corinth probably carried the greatest resemblance to the church
in America. Thus, Paul's message to the Corinthian church is especially relevant to the American church.

A Current Message For America

Listen, America—pay attention to the message of 1 and 2
Corinthians!

There is an emphasis in 1 & 2 Corinthians that speaks strongly
to us today. This theme is present in some of Paul's other epistles,
but not with the same frequency and intensity.

I am referring to Paul's emphasis on dying for the sake of the
gospel. The letters to Corinth contain the bulk of Paul's "theology
of death." This is not the death to sin that Romans deals with. This
is a death to good things, to normal things, to healthy things — all
for the sake of the extension of the kingdom.

Paul didn't have to talk to the Thessalonians about dying. Through the extreme persecution they faced, the Thessalonians knew a lot already about dying. But he did talk to the prosperous Corinthians about dying.

The Corinthian believers — man, they were living. They had one of the most exciting churches going. They had freedom, energy, and momentum. And it's to this church that Paul writes about death.

Here are the primary verses from Corinthians which represent Paul's theology of death:

- You are already full! You are already rich! You have reigned as kings without us—and indeed I could wish you did reign, that we also might reign with you! For I think that God has displayed us, the apostles, last, as men condemned to death; for we have been made a spectacle to the world, both to angels and to men (1 Corinthians 4:8-9).
- I affirm, by the boasting in you which I have in Christ Jesus our Lord, I die daily (1 Corinthians 15:31).
- For we do not want you to be ignorant, brethren, of our trouble which came to us in Asia: that we were burdened beyond measure, above strength, so that we despaired even of life. Yes, we had the sentence of death in ourselves, that we should not trust in ourselves but in God who raises the dead, who delivered us from so great a death, and does deliver us; in whom we trust that He will still deliver us (2 Corinthians 1:8-10).
- Always carrying about in the body the dying of the Lord Jesus, that the life of Jesus also may be manifested in our body. For we who live are always delivered to death for Jesus' sake, that the life of Jesus also may be manifested in our mortal flesh. So then death is working in us, but life in you (2 Corinthians 4:10-12).
- As unknown, and yet well known; as dying, and behold we live; as chastened, and yet not killed (2 Corinthians 6:9).

Paul's message in these verses must catch the ear of American believers today. Paul is saying, "You have so much; you are rich financially and rich in teaching. Already you are reigning in this life. The difference between you and us apostles is, we're still laying our lives down for the gospel. Death is working in our lives on a daily basis, while you bask in the wealth of your attainments in Christ. Is this the time to enjoy your comforts in Christ when others have not yet heard the gospel? No, my friends, this is not a time to live; this is a time to die. This is a time to lay your lives down for the cause of Christ."

That's why Paul says, "Therefore, I urge you, imitate me" (1 Corinthians 4:16). I have been gripped and convicted personally at how little my life resembles Paul's. He described his lifestyle in this way: "To the present hour we both hunger and thirst, and we are poorly clothed, and beaten, and homeless" (1 Corinthians 4:11). What will it take for my life to be described with those same words? Nothing short of a radical embracing of Christ's call to the cross.

There is no greater way we can express the fiery intensity of our love for Christ than to lay our lives down for the sake of the gospel.

5

SHARING IN HIS SUFFERINGS

Wanting To Suffer

Look again at Philippians 3:10, "that I may know Him and the power of His resurrection, and the fellowship of His sufferings, being conformed to His death." In saying, "that I may know...the fellowship of His sufferings," Paul is essentially saying, "I **want** to suffer." He's saying, "As much as I want to know Christ and the power of His resurrection, I also want to share in Christ's sufferings."

"Why, Paul? Why would you want to suffer? Are you a masochist?"

"No," Paul would respond. "I don't enjoy pain. I'm not motivated toward pain, but I am motivated toward Him. **I want to know Him!** And I realize that the only way to get to know Him is by sharing in the fellowship of His sufferings, being conformed to His death."

Wow! Paul wasn't simply talking about a **willingness** to embrace suffering ("Lord, I'm willing to suffer, if it should be Your will"), but he actually spoke of a **longing** to share in Christ's sufferings.

Paul was basically saying, "Bring on the pain! Let me suffer! Let's get on with it!" Not because he was a self-mutilator, but because he had an overwhelming cry in his heart to get to know Christ better.

Paul had a revelation of the love of Christ! And for as much as He saw, He realized there was so much more revelation to be had.

So he said, "To gain more of that love, I will run into the crucified life." He had become addicted to a love that would lead him to his death. I can hear the great apostle crying, "I'll do **anything** to gain this love of Christ!"

"Being conformed to his death" (Phil. 3:10). The goal of my life should be to approximate more and more the agony of His cross. Just look at His cross, at His bloody, convulsing figure—who do you know, among all His followers, that comes close to resembling that picture? We look more like Barabbas than Jesus. Like Barabbas, we've been set free, and we carry our banners through the streets, celebrating our freedom—while Jesus hangs alone on the cross. "The sting of death is gone!" we sing, and like Barabbas we walk away from the cross, free. Is there enough gratefulness and love in our hearts to return (like the Samaritan leper) and identify with Jesus in His passion?

In times past, I have had a wrong concept of the cross. I've seen Christ's work on the cross as being totally substitutionary, as though Christ suffered for us so that we don't have to suffer. To be sure, His work of redemption on the cross was entirely substitutionary—He took our place on the cross so that we never have to experience the wrath of God against sin. Believing in Christ exempts us from God's wrath, and in that sense Christ's cross is absolutely substitutionary. **But His suffering on the cross did not exempt us from suffering**. Rather, He invites us to participate in the suffering of His cross. He invites us to be so drawn by the love displayed on His cross that we respond in love by **desiring** to take up our cross.

Love **wants** to share the cross. Love doesn't look at the cross and say, "Thank you, Jesus, for suffering so that I never have to suffer." Love looks at the cross and says, "Oh, how can I share this moment with You, Lord? How can I identify with You in Your pain? Is there a way that You and I can do this together? Can we be partners in life, and partners in death? You are my Betrothed, and I want to be with You in **everything** to which Your Father calls You."

We avoid the cross because we're stupid. We try to avert the pain, little realizing exactly what we're running from. We don't understand the love that the cross opens before us. **The cross be-**

comes the most generous offer God could make—an opportunity for us to love Jesus with the same fiery intensity with which He loves us. You thought you knew love—until you took up the cross. To the one who takes up his cross, there comes a flood of unparalleled affection from the Lamb who was slain. "You would do this for Me?" the Lord asks. "You would suffer in this way because you love Me so much?" Nothing touches the Lamb's heart like this kind of love.

Why do we have such an aversion to persecution when Jesus said the reward in heaven for the persecuted is great? (See Matthew 5:12.) Why do we seek out the path of least resistance rather than the way of the cross? It is because we have convoluted values. We don't want to witness to our neighbors because of the reproach and rejection we might experience, even though Jesus promised a great reward to those who are thus rejected. Why do we avoid the promise of great reward?

Learning Obedience Through Suffering

The Book of Hebrews says this about Jesus:

Though He was a Son, yet He learned obedience by the things which He suffered. And having been perfected, He became the author of eternal salvation to all who obey Him (Hebrews 5:8-9).

The way of obedience is painful. One reason many don't walk in obedience is because they evade the suffering that obedience often necessitates. They don't understand that on the other side of the suffering is the greatest fulfillment man can realize.

Jesus was perfect, yet He learned obedience. He learned obedience as the Son of Man. Never before had He lived as a Man, and so He was learning what it meant to walk in obedience as a Man. Jesus was always perfect — He was a perfect baby, a perfect teen, a perfect adult. But he was not perfected until He had suffered. Bob Mumford illustrates it this way: an acorn is perfect; an oak tree is perfected.

The New Testament word for "obedience" is very intriguing. A compound word in the Greek language, it means literally, "to hear under."

Thus, to be obedient is not simply to hear. I can hear and then choose to disobey. To obey — "to hear under" — is to hear with an attitude of submission. Obedience is a positional thing. I bring my life under God's rule and submit myself to everything I hear. So obedience involves coming under God's authority.

Jesus learned obedience perfectly. That means He heard from His Father with an attitude of full submission. He complied with everything He heard because His life was totally surrendered to His Father's will.

Jesus' life illustrates this important kingdom principle: You don't have to fail in order to learn. Jesus never failed once as He learned obedience. When I saw this, I became so excited. I realized I had believed a lie. I thought I couldn't learn without first blowing it. But now I see that if I'm living in a place of submission to the Father, I can learn to hear Him and obey Him without ever having to fail. The key is in hearing from a heart of submission. That's why the Holy Spirit is saying so forcefully to us in this hour: "Listen!"

Obedience Produces Suffering

The place of obedience is the safest place in the universe to be, and it's also the most dangerous place to be. The closer we follow Christ, the safer we are, but the more abuse we experience. We're safe because we're in His will, but we're hurting because we're encountering so many obstacles and challenges.

One of the passions of the holy life is to find the place of safety "under the shadow of the Almighty" (Psalm 91:1). This is the painful dilemma of Psalm 91. As we press into the shelter of the shadow of the Almighty, we find some of the most painful things coming into our lives. We cry for protection, but it seems that the more passionately we pursue Him, the more flak we face. Jesus warned us of this, of course, when He said they would hate us because they hated Him. The closer we draw to Christ, the more hate we encounter.

By appearances, the one who dwells in the secret place of the Most High encounters more hassles than ever. According to externals, that's true. But the one who dwells in the secret place of the Most High doesn't live by externals — he lives by the inward life of the Spirit. Therefore, while his body and soul may be afflicted with harassment and abuse, the spirit of the saint has found a place of protection under the shadow of the Almighty where he is beyond all injury — it is the place of immunity.

This truth is seen in the lives of many saints. Take Moses. The closer he drew in to the will of God in leading the nation of Israel, the more flak he faced, both from Pharaoh and also from his fellow Israelites.

Take David. The closer he came to entering into his calling as king of Israel, the hotter the attacks on him grew, both from Saul and his own ranks.

Take Jesus. As He walked faithfully toward the cross, the opposition continuously escalated, to the point of death.

The place of obedience is simultaneously the place of greatest protection and greatest abuse. Some saints, in an effort to save their life, have shied away from the opposition and hate they've had to face. What they did not realize is that by averting the pain, they left their first love — the shadow of the Almighty. The external opposition became more liveable, but they lost the secret place of inner protection.

Read Psalm 91 again, and see if the secret place of internal refuge is not in fact the place of escalating external attack. As the attacks increase, the saint cries, "Hide me!" The Spirit thus draws him into a place of greater spiritual peace and comfort, which only inflames his soul with a greater passion for Jesus, which in turn only feeds the ire of his tormentors. Make the decision now: Lose your life, and pursue the secret place of the Most High. It is the way of the cross.

The Cross: Gateway To Glory

The Father and the Spirit have this certain fixation, this preoccupation, to establish the Son — the Lamb who was obedient to death — as the focal point of the universe. He is center stage. The only way to honor the Father is to honor the Son He sent.

In discussing the plan of redemption, I can suppose at some point in eternity past the Father saying, "Son, if you will become the Lamb, there will be incredible pain and humiliation for you; but there will also be, subsequent to that suffering, greater glory than this universe has ever seen. You will be the recipient of untold glory." How could the Father bestow even greater glory on the Son than He already had, since He already shared equality with God? This greater glory will come from the saints — the Bride. "Give Him glory, all you people." Christ's obedience to the cross is bringing to Him incredible glory from the Bride, from the Lamb's wife, a people who were created for His glory.

What is true for Jesus is also true for us: **the greatest glory is opened up only to those who embrace the cross**.

Jesus understood His Father's love and knew that the Father inflicted pain in order to produce a greater glory. What glory is now ascribed to Him who was willing to embrace the suffering of death! No one has known pain like Christ. He's looking for a Bride with whom He can relate, who can identify with His joys and who has also experienced His pains. Do you really want to be like Christ? You must embrace the hand of the Father; you must embrace the cross. To do so is to abandon yourself with open arms to your heavenly Father, receiving the cup He gives you, and losing your will in His. From this abandonment will rise a Bride worthy of the name of Jesus Christ.

You'll never get to know the cross academically. If you pray, "Lord, show me Your cross," you're probably praying more than you realize. He doesn't just reveal His cross, He works it in you. The cross is learned experiencially.

When Jesus said, "My food is to do the will of Him who sent Me, and to finish His work" (John 4:34), He was making an overt reference to His cross. This was the work He was to finish. Even though He hungered and thirsted on the cross, He nevertheless said, "This is my food; my sustenance is here, in laying my life down, because it is My Father's will." O glorious attainment, when the suffering we endure becomes our food, for we know it is the will of God. "Father, I am willing to walk out my present pathway through the most torturous, difficult route, if You so will — because Your will is my life, my sustenance, my survival."

The Crucified Lover

When Jesus was on the cross, He gave Himself to one thing. There He hung. The awareness of His Father's presence that He had always enjoyed had suddenly disappeared. The very people He had come to serve were maliciously and vindictively torturing Him to death. And besides all that, He sustained the wrath of God as He took the punishment for our sins. But He just hung there — **and loved God!**

All Jesus did on the cross, in spite of the total injustice of His suffering, was to love His Father.

And now here comes a Bride. She is longing to share this moment of suffering with her Beloved. And as she takes up her cross and suffers unjustly before God and man, all she is doing is loving her Lord. God looks at this Bride and says, "Son, she reminds me of You. That's exactly what You did. She's just loving Me in the midst of her pain."

And the Son says, ""Father, now I see it—**this** is the Bride You promised Me. You said she'd be like Me. You told Me I would be able to relate to her. You said we'd have things in common that we would be able to share for all eternity. You said she would be My co-equal partner. And oh, My Father, she is...why, she's...**beautiful!**"

"Yes, she certainly is beautiful," replies the Father. "When You went to the cross, You moved My heart so, My Son. I never thought anything could ever again move My heart like that. But now as I behold her, sharing in Your sufferings, I must say that My heart is moved all over again. She is absolutely amazing to Me. For as much as I love You, My Son, I love her too!"

Section Three

MOTIVATIONS OF THE HEART

6

PURIFIED HEART MOTIVATIONS

One reason so many believers are "going through the fire" right now is because God is in the business of purifying the most inner motivations of our hearts. He wants us to serve Him because we love Him, not because we love accomplishments or love to see the fruit of our labors.

To change the motivations of the human heart is no small thing, and only God can do it. No matter how hard we might try, we can never change the fundamental motives that drive our actions. We are able with our willpower to adapt our behavior to a limited degree, but we are powerless to change our motivations.

Our motivations are shaped by a variety of factors from the moment of conception, and to change something that is so deeply rooted in the very essence of who we've come to be is impossible—except for God.

God is not interested simply in what we do, or how we serve Him; He is deeply interested in why we do what we do. He's not only looking for pure actions but pure motives. Therefore, He applies the fire of His love to our life—and it comes in the form of crisis, pain, distress, or calamity. The calamity is actually an instrument of His love, designed to purify and change us to become more like Jesus.

The purifying of our motives is essential because our eternal reward will be directly related to the motives in which we served.

We can do great exploits for God, but if our motive is not love, it profits us nothing (see Matthew 7:22-23).

Jeremiah 17:9-10 says that the motives of men's hearts are extremely deceitful, and we don't know our own hearts. But the Lord searches men's hearts and will "give every man according to his ways, according to the fruit of his doings."

There are times when we actually start to feel fairly spiritual and feel like we're really starting to get a handle on this thing called Christianity. Then, God just pulls back a little corner of our hearts, and reveals to us our true motivations. "Ugh!" we say. "Where did that ugly thing come from, Lord?" We discover there is iniquity in our hearts regarding which we are completely oblivious, so the Lord calls us to a commitment of increasingly purifying the motives of our hearts.

As God has turned up the fire in my life, I have come to recognize four heart motivations that He is seeking to cultivate in my life. As you review these four motivations of the heart, I trust you will receive confirmation and clarity regarding what God is doing in your life at this time. He is looking for everything we do to spring from these four great heart desires:

> "I want to be with Him."
> "I want to know Him."
> "I want to please Him."
> "I want His honor."

7

I WANT TO BE WITH HIM

The first passion that moves everything we do is right here: "Lord, I've just got to be with You, wherever You are!" Christians are known by one common denominator: They have this passion to hang out with Jesus. They just want to follow the Lamb around wherever He goes.

Even as this cry erupts from our soul, "O Lord, I want to be with You!" we discover something: He's always on the move!

The Scriptures are consistent in portraying this quality of our Lord Jesus. In the Song of Solomon He is described as "leaping upon the mountains, skipping upon the hills" (Song of Solomon 2:8). In the Bible, "mountains" primarily represent two things: great obstacles (e.g., Mark 11:23), and nations or spheres of human authority (e.g., Isaiah 2:2). In a figurative sense, then, this verse describes Jesus as bounding effortlessly over every challenge and problem that this fallen world might present, and it also portrays Him as moving victoriously through the nations. He is the reigning King of the nations!

This image is reinforced in the Book of Revelation where Jesus is seen as a rider on a white horse who goes forth through the nations, victoriously conquering His foes (see Revelation 6:2; 19:11). Jesus has an agenda for the entire world, and so He rides through the nations to conquer the hearts of men and women with His love.

When we look at Jesus in the gospel stories, this quality of Jesus is vividly clear. He is constantly on the move. Actually, to be one of Jesus' followers and to keep up with Him, you had to be fairly fit. He was constantly walking from village to village, spending many hours on the road, taking the gospel to people who had not heard.

So when we pray, "Lord, I want to follow You. I just want to be where You are," we quickly realize that in order to stay in Christ's shadow we've got to keep pace with Him. His heart is for the needy masses of the world, and we will not be able to stay in His company if we isolate ourselves and take up permanent residence in our prayer closet. **If we want to be with Him, we're going to have to go with Him to touch the needs of the people of the world.**

Paul's Motivations

Paul talks about his heart motivations in the third chapter of Philippians. Look at these two verses:

> Brethren, I do not count myself to have apprehended; but one thing I do, forgetting those things which are behind and reaching forward to those things which are ahead, I press toward the goal for the prize of the upward call of God in Christ Jesus (Philippians 3:13-14).

In these verses, I believe Paul is telling us what moves him to travel from nation to nation.

When I've looked at Paul's life, sometimes I've been tempted to think that he may have been almost hyper. He strikes me like one of those guys who is wired to 220 volts. You know the type— they don't need much sleep, they're constantly on the go, and they can never just slow down and relax a little. Some people are high-energy types, and they attack life with gusto. I thought maybe Paul was just one of those kinds of people. Maybe that's what motivated Paul to travel constantly from nation to nation, I conjectured. Maybe it was just because he couldn't sit still.

But Paul helps us to understand what drove Him. He says that it's "the upward call of God in Christ Jesus." When I look at how Paul travelled internationally, I would have expected him to say "the **outward** call of God in Christ Jesus." I was ready for him to say, "God has called me to go **out** to the nations, so I must obey that outward call." But instead, Paul talks about an "upward call."

Paul is saying, "I've been called of God to come **up**. Christ is bidding me to come higher, to ascend to a higher level of relationship with Himself. He is calling me to get to know Him better."

"But," Paul would add, "I've discovered something. If I want to gain Christ, if I want to know Him better, if I want to be with Him—it doesn't happen in a corner. I've come to realize that Jesus is constantly on the move, running in the nations. And if I'm going to stay with Him, I've got to be on the move as well."

The thing that motivated Paul was not an enjoyment of international travel, but it was an overwhelming urgency to stay in pace with His beloved Lord. He just wanted to be with Jesus, and if that meant getting on a boat, or travelling by road, he was willing to do it.

Intimacy Versus Ministry Accomplishments

The Lord is completely transforming our motivations. He is searching our hearts and revealing what it is that motivates us to "leap upon mountains" with Jesus in servant ministry.

He is asking us, "Are you motivated by the 'rush' of accomplishing exploits in My name?" It is the natural tendency of our flesh to be energized when we see our efforts accomplishing tangible results for the kingdom of God. How we exult when someone gets saved or healed or delivered through our ministry! How we are warmed when someone expresses appreciation for our labors. But it is a carnal and impure motivation.

Jesus is saying, "How I desire that you be motivated by the sheer delight of being with Me!"

When we serve Jesus simply because we long to be with Him and to be doing what He's doing, then the question for us becomes, "Where are You today for me, Lord Jesus?" If for me Jesus is at work, I want to be at work; if for me He is at home, I want to be home; if for me He is reaching out to the people of my community, then I want to be on the streets with Him. I just want to be where He is—because I love Him so much.

Listen, dear reader: if Jesus is sprawled on your couch watching TV, by all means join Him! (Get it?)

Our responsibility is simply to be where He is and to do what He's doing.

Sometimes we plan our ministry activities, and then we hope and pray for God's blessing. Instead of planning first and praying second, I'm wondering what would happen if we inverted the order. What would happen if we first of all sought Him and found out where He was and what He was doing? If we gave ourselves to doing what He is doing, then we wouldn't have to plead with Him to bless our efforts. Our labors would be automatically blessed because we would be working with Him. If we did our praying up front, I believe we'd enter a greater dimension of kingdom fruitfulness. Instead of begging God to bless our ideas, we would be giving ourselves to those things that are prompted by the heart of God.

If you're serving because you want to see souls saved, you'll probably get discouraged and quit. **If, however, your motivation is to be with Jesus, then you'll never weary of reaching out to human needs. You'll be energized by the joy of fellowship with the Lord Jesus in the midst of the harvest field.**

Let this cry fill your heart just now: "Lord, I just want to be with You!"

8

I WANT TO KNOW HIM

The first motivation of my heart is that I want to be with Him. And the reason I want to be with Him is this: I want to know Him! This is the second great motivation that I want to energize all that I do. I want to know Him "in whom are hidden all the treasures of wisdom and knowledge" (Colossians 2:3).

This is the passion that fills the breast of the saint who has been quickened to the beauty of Christ's face. Above all else, he longs desperately to know more of Christ.

Hebrews 3:3 says the builder of a house has more honor than the house itself. Speaking of Christ, the writer is saying that the Creator of the universe has more honor than the universe itself. Jesus is more honorable, more glorious, more incredible than the universe He created! So take your pick of the created order—want to tour a far-off galaxy? Interested in exploring a supernova? As splendiferous as that may be, exploring the face of Jesus is even more exciting!

Moses Wanted To Know Him

On one occasion Moses prayed, "Please, show me your glory" (Exodus 33:18). To understand this request, let me give you some background.

I don't know anyone, apart from Jesus Himself, who had so many encounters with the glory of God. Look at the list:

1. He sees a burning bush.
2. His rod turns to a serpent, and his hand becomes leprous then whole.
3. He sees the ten plagues on Egypt.
4. He watches the Red Sea part, the people cross over on dry ground, and then he sees Pharaoh's army drown in the sea.
5. He sees the glory of God come upon Mt. Sinai. There's lightning, thunder, a thick cloud, a piercing trumpet blast, the whole mountain is shaking and burning with smoke billowing from it like a furnace. Then at God's command he ascends the mountain **into** the billowing inferno.
6. After being in that glory with God on the mountain for 40 days, he comes down, takes care of business, and then ascends for a second set of 40 days. It is during this time that the glory of God is so completely upon him that he doesn't realize it, but his face is glistening with the radiance of God's glory. And it's at this point that Moses prays, "Please, show me your glory."

I'm sort of surprised that God wasn't disgusted with this request. "You ingrate!" I would have imagined God to retort, "After all the glory I've shown you, you want more?" But God didn't respond like that. Instead, it's obvious that God was delighted by this request. Even though Moses had already known more glory in his life than any other human, God was pleased that he would want to see even more of His glory.

Moses had his priorities in good order. Above all, he wanted to know God. This desire to know Him was rewarded by God, and it's a desire that God is still rewarding today.

O To Know Him!

The Lord said through the prophet Hosea, "My people are destroyed for lack of knowledge" (Hosea 4:6). Great poverty and destruction has come to the church because of a lack of knowledge. But it's not simply a lack of Bible knowledge. It's not saying, "Because you don't know the Scriptures." If you look at the context (specifically verse 1), Hosea is talking about the "knowledge of God." God is saying, "You are impoverished because you don't know Me." O the riches and blessing of coming to know God!

To know God was the great passion that captivated the heart of Paul. He wrote, "Yet indeed I also count all things loss for the excellence of the knowledge of Christ Jesus my Lord, for whom I have suffered the loss of all things, and count them as rubbish, that I may gain Christ" (Philippians 3:8).

Paul had been granted a revelation of Jesus Christ, and he knew there was infinitely more to attain. He had experienced the sheer delight of having the Holy Spirit reveal the glory of God that's in the face of Christ.

In the previous verses, Paul has just listed his earthly attainments—a Hebrew of the Hebrews, a Pharisee, concerning the Law blameless, etc. But he says he willfully lost all that in exchange for the glory of getting to know Christ. In fact, when he compares his past attainments to the glory of gaining Christ, he calls his previous attainments "rubbish." Paul is saying, "Don't even talk to me about what I had to give up to become a Christian. It's nothing; it's garbage; it's rubbish. What I have given up is totally non-significant in the light of the glory that I have gained in getting to know Jesus Christ."

Unparalleled Pleasure

There is nothing as glorious to the human heart as the revelation of Jesus Christ to one's understanding. When the glory of God comes upon you, and the Holy Spirit fills you, expanding your heart with fresh revelation of the incredible love of Christ—that is an unequalled pleasure. Every other pursuit becomes a paltry and cheap substitute. We were created to know Christ.

People pursue pleasure in other places, never realizing that they are rejecting the fountain of all joy and delight. We have been invited to drink from the eternal fountain of God's love. For the saint, the thrill of eternity will be the never-ending unfolding of the beauty and glory of Christ Jesus.

I want to know Him—because there is no one like Him! He is absolutely unparalleled in wonder and excellence. Even God said,

"I know of no other besides Me" (see Isaiah 44:8). There isn't even a close second. And He has invited us to behold Him who is altogether lovely.

He is so wonderful and magnificent that the sheer beauty of His person casts off an aura which we call "the glory of God." The glory of God is the radiation that emanates from His presence. It is an energy field that derives its life from the sheer splendor of Him who is seated on the Throne. **And yet the glory of God is but a manifestation and a reflection of something that far exceeds this glory—His person.**

The Essence Of God

I have wondered, "What is the most fundamental attribute of God's nature?" Someone might suggest, "In the very essence of His being, God is love." When we say that God's foremost quality is love, however, we get into a lot of trouble. There are many people who misunderstand the judgments of God because they believe that God's over-arching quality is that of love. "How could a God of love send people to hell?" they ask. They don't understand that God is not only love, God is holy.

"That's it," someone else might suggest. "God's most fundamental quality is that He is holy." I used to believe that myself, until I began to entertain another thought. **Let me suggest, for your meditation, that God's most intrinsic quality is that He is beautiful.** Every other quality emanates from His beauty, which means that every other quality of His nature is also beautiful.

Psalm 96:9 says, "Worship the Lord in the beauty of holiness," which suggests to me that His beauty is fundamental to holiness.

When David says He longs to gaze upon the beauty of the Lord (Psalm 27:4), He is saying that He delights to behold the very essence of God.

The Altogether Beautiful One

God the Father esteems the Son and considers all beauty to reside in Him. A thing is beautiful only if God says so. If it's beautiful to God, it's beautiful. Sin has distorted our ability to perceive beauty. The regenerate man is awakened to appreciate the beauty of God.

There is not a moment in Jesus' history when He was not altogether beautiful. Even on the cross—and especially on the cross—He was an altogether beautiful sacrifice to God.

When you clothe yourself with the Lord Jesus (see Colossians 3), you take on the beauty of God Himself. This is the ultimate incentive to holiness. The saint who is clothed with holiness turns the head of Jesus. We want to grow in holiness because we want to become increasingly attractive to Jesus.

As Moses cried, "Let the beauty of the Lord our God be upon us!" (Psalm 90:17).

Again, the wonder and glory of all this is simply this: I have been invited into a relationship in which I will forever be giving myself to knowing more and more about the beauty and splendor of my Beloved, the altogether Lovely One, the one who contains the fullness of the beauty of God.

Let my every endeavor spring from this motivation: "Lord, I want to know You!"

Intimacy In Service

When you're running with Jesus in active service, He reveals Himself to you. This becomes the reward of serving at the side of Christ. The reward is not seeing ministry results, but in getting to know Him more fully.

There is a dimension of Jesus you'll never know until you accompany Him into the harvest. If you really want to know Him, you're going to have to work with Him in the fields which are ripe for harvesting.

When you're working with Jesus in the harvest, you see His love for mankind. You see the glint in His eye as He brings His own unto Himself. And you receive the love that He reserves for those who have made His interests their interests. Jesus withholds certain aspects of His beauty from common view, but He discloses Himself to the one who will go with Him to the harvest.

Our reaching out to the world will never be pure until we move past a love for people and touch them because of a consuming passion to know Jesus. The reason we don't shine for Jesus as we should is because we don't love Him as we should. The intensity of our witness is directly proportional to the intensity of our love. Our problem is not fear of rejection (from people); our problem is apathy (toward Jesus). When we fervently long to know Christ, we will obey His command to "go into all the world" because we'll understand that the place of active service is the place where we're going to get to know Him better.

We are to love the sinners whom God is calling to Himself just as much as we love those who have already believed. God is reserving a baptism of love for His last-days Church that will transform her into a fiery blaze of passionate concern for the lost. No amount of rejection will be able to extinguish this fire for the lost because the intensity of the fire is in no way regulated by people's responses, but by the love of God being shed abroad in the heart. You can pour as much water on a burning oil well as you might want; you're not going to extinguish the flame because it's being fed by an underground supply. The only way to stop the flame is to cut off the inner supply. **Evangelistic efforts fueled by people's responses are sure to fizzle out; evangelistic fervor that is fueled by God's love from within can face any human or demonic obstacle without diminishment**.

The Desires Of Christ

Just before His death, Jesus opened up His heart in the presence of His disciples and expressed the deepest prayers of His soul to God. He cried, "Father, I desire that they also whom You gave Me may be with Me where I am, that they may behold My glory which You have given Me; for You loved Me before the foundation of the world" (John 17:24).

Jesus wanted His disciples to overhear this prayer. There are times, especially in the presence of our family members, when it is very appropriate to let others overhear the deepest prayers of our heart. Your kids need to hear your heart passion before God!

In their presence Jesus prayed, "I desire." Such a statement must arrest our attention. Here is God, the Second Person of the Trinity, about to express His great desire. What will it be? What desires motive the heart of God?

The Greek word for "desire" is "*thelo*," and it means: to determine, make a positive choice; by implication, to will, wish, or desire. The word is usually translated "will" in the King James Version, as it expresses desire and purpose.

In just an hour or so Jesus is going to the garden of Gethsemane, and He is going to defer to His Father's will. He is going to say, "Not what I *thelo* [will, desire, purpose], but what You *thelo*, Father." This was an expression of absolute surrender to His Father's will.

The Father's *thelo* was that Jesus be crucified, and Jesus was willing to submit to that. But here Jesus expresses **His** *thelo*. In John 17:24 Jesus is saying, "Father, here's My passion, My *thelo*. First of all, I *thelo* (desire) that they may be with Me where I am. And secondly, I *thelo* (desire) that they may behold My glory."

The two primary motivations of Jesus' heart are the two heart motivations that we've discussed so far. Here's what drives Jesus' heart: He just wants us to be with Him, and He just wants us to know Him— to behold His glory.

The Bride is on earth, crying, "Lord, I just want to be with You," and the Bridegroom is in heaven, saying, "And I just want you to be with Me." The Bride is on earth, panting, "Oh, I just want to know You, Lord, to see you in Your glory," and the Bridegroom is in heaven, declaring, "That's all I want, too. I just want you to see My glory, and to know who I really am." The same bridal cry erupts from both parties as they look ahead with great anticipation to that day when they will be together, forever.

May the desires that fill the heart of our beloved Bridegroom also be the desires that motivate our hearts!

9

I WANT TO PLEASE HIM

This is the third great motivation that fills the heart of the one who is abandoned to God's purposes. Above all else he wants to please the Lord Jesus.

David wrote, "I delight to do Your will, O my God" (Psalm 40:8). O the delight of doing God's will and God's will alone! It is called "abandoned obedience."

How sweet it is, when you **know** that you're doing God's will. It is so precious when the Father gently whispers to your heart, "You are My beloved son, in whom I am well pleased."

Well Pleasing To God

The Father spoke those words over His Son when Jesus was baptized by John at the Jordan River (Matthew 3:17). It's interesting to note that as yet Jesus had not healed anyone, cast out any demons, or preached the gospel to anyone. All He had done to that point in His earthly walk was stay at home, take care of His mother, and love His Father. And yet the Father says, "You are My beloved Son, in whom I am well pleased." In terms of kingdom business Jesus had to that point done absolutely nothing, and yet the Father was "well pleased" with Him.

Applied to our lives, this truth reveals that God's pleasure over our lives has very little to do with the kinds of exploits we're doing for Him. If you're seeking to please Him by working real hard for Him, you're missing it big time. The thing that pleases God is a heart that loves Him extravagantly, even if you're in a season of stillness.

In fact, sometimes the Lord will test our hearts by forcing us to quit an area of fruitful ministry. Here we are, serving God and loving it; and many people's lives are being touched and changed through our ministry. Then here comes God, and He pulls the carpet out from under us and everything stops. The Christian's worst nightmare. It's not until God takes away our ministry that we usually see the true motives of our hearts. While we're functional we think our motives are so pure. But when God removes us from ministry, suddenly we find things surfacing in our hearts that we never knew were there. We find ourselves discontented and chafing under the divinely ordained restrictions.

Then the Lord comes to us: "Why are you so upset? You've still got Me. Am I not enough for you? Or do you also need your ministry in order to be fulfilled?"

The Lord is jealous enough over us to purify our love. He wants us to love Him with all our hearts, even when we're on the shelf in terms of ministry activity. This is the thing that pleases His heart—an affectionate devotion that is expressed totally independently of all external circumstances.

Longing To Please Him

To please God was the great cry of Paul: "Therefore we make it our aim, whether present or absent, to be well pleasing to Him" (2 Corinthians 5:9). Paul also wrote, "For do I now persuade men, or God? Or do I seek to please men? For if I still pleased men, I would not be a bondservant of Christ" (Galatians 1:10). In this verse Paul establishes this principle: **We are to please God and persuade men—not (as we're often inclined) to persuade God and please men.**

The Rewards Of Pleasing God

The Scriptures give us several incentives to please God. I would like to point to four verses.

1. By this I know that You are well pleased with me, because my enemy does not triumph over me (Psalm
   41:11).

   This verse tells us that God will not allow those who
   please Him to be overcome by their enemies. He will
   fight for them and deliver them. Now, that's a great
   promise! But there's more.

2. And whatever we ask we receive from Him, because we
   keep His commandments and do those things that are
   pleasing in His sight (1 John 3:22).

   This verse says that when we please Him we will receive the answers to our prayers. Now, that ain't bad!
   There are some prayers that I'd like to have answered,
   so I think I'll pursue this thing of pleasing God. But
   there's more.

3. "And He who sent Me is with Me. The Father has not
   left Me alone, for I always do those things that please
   Him" (John 8:29).

   Jesus said He enjoyed uninterrupted fellowship with the
   Father because He always pleased His Father. This is
   the delightful norm of everyday living for the one who
   pleases God—he enjoys continual companionship with
   God. But there's even more.

4. "He who has My commandments and keeps them, it is
   he who loves Me. And he who loves Me will be loved
   by My Father, and I will love him and manifest Myself
   to him" (John 14:21).

Above all, I want to please Him because I want to inherit the
promise of John 14:21. These words are filled with meaning.
   • "He who has My commandments"—Jesus isn't simply

saying, "He who owns a Bible." It's not enough to have a
written copy of His commandments on your person. Jesus
is describing the person who studies and pursues His commandments and is not satisfied until they are such an ab-
sorbed part of his heart that he owns the words of Jesus.
We ought to absorb every portion of Scripture in that way,
but I have chosen to take this statement very literally and
to give myself specifically to taking in the words of Jesus
Himself. I want to give the best of my time and energies
to ingesting and living the words that Jesus spoke when
He was on the earth.

- "and keeps them"—It's not enough to have His commandments, to know them, or to even be able to teach about
  them. Above all, we must obey His words.

- "it is he who loves Me"—This is the litmus test for loving God. **The one who chases down Jesus' words, takes
  them fervently into his heart, and then diligently
  adapts his lifestyle in order to adhere to Christ's
  words—Jesus said this is the one who loves Him.** When
  we sing our love songs to Jesus, but know we are living
  in disobedience to His will, we are deceiving ourselves.
  If I really love Him, I will devote myself to doing His
  commandments.

- "And he who loves Me will be loved by My Father"—
  This is the reward of pleasing God: the Father will lavish
  His love upon you. What greater reward could there possibly be? God the Father will surround you with His affections, and He will whisper to your heart just how much
  He loves you. This is worth sacrificing all else for. This
  is worth being obedient even unto death. **It can't get
  any better than this—to be the recipient of the passionate, boundless, fiery love of the Father**.

- "and I will love him"—Wait a moment, it just got better!
  **If I walk in abandoned obedience, not only will the
  Father pour His limitless love upon me, but the Lord
  Jesus will also shower His love upon me!** He is the one
  who has won my heart; He is my betrothed; He is the

only one I want to behold; I only have eyes for Him; I would do **anything** for His love. And here He tells me that He **will** love me. For this I have forsaken all; for this I have embraced self-denial; for this I have taken up my cross. And now that which I have panted after is actually being extended to me. To be the object of His ineffable love—it doesn't get any better than this!

- "and manifest Myself to him"—Hold on, I can't believe it—it just got even better! **If I walk in abandoned obedience, not only will the Father pour His limitless love upon me, and not only will Jesus lavish His affection upon me, but He will reveal Himself to me in a most singular and vivid way.** That settles it, folks. My heart is a goner. I'm won. I am owned, I'm a bondslave to this love. To have Jesus manifest Himself to me? I'd do **anything** for that! Just to behold Him! He is the altogether lovely one; He is the fairest of ten thousand; He is the subject of angel's songs; He transfigures the universe with the brightness of His glory; He is the fullness of the Godhead bodily; He is the perfection of beauty. And here He promises to manifest Himself to me, in the fullness of His glory and majesty. There's no contest—nothing else comes remotely close. What can compare to seeing His face? To gazing into His fiery eyes? To hearing His majestic voice? To receiving the kisses of His mouth? To beholding the shining glory of His countenance? The pursuit of this glory has become the consuming passion of my very existence.

So now my heart cries, "Lord, the only thing I want to do is please You! Help me, Lord, to know the things that touch Your heart. Help me to know how to please You, even as You pleased Your Father."

10

I WANT HIS HONOR

This is the fourth motivation that is the driving force behind all that I do. I do what I do because I want to receive the honor that God will bestow in the last day upon those who do His will.

God wants us to be motivated by a passionate desire to receive His honor, rather than being motivated to receive the honor of man. **The honor of God is "the prize" toward which we strain.** More than anything else, I press toward the goal of hearing the Lord Jesus say to me on that final day, "Well done, good and faithful servant." That one word of honor from His lips will have made every hassle and difficulty here on earth worth it.

Greatly Beloved

I find Daniel's life story most gripping. He models for us what it means to seek God's honor, even when men would lavish their honor upon us.

I want to highlight one specific story in Daniel's history, but to do so I need to lay down a backdrop. Twice Daniel is told by a heavenly messenger that he is "greatly beloved" by God (Daniel 10:11,19). This is said to Daniel with great emphasis. In essence he is told, "Daniel, God **really** has a thing for you. Of all the men on earth, you are the recipient of an unusual and most profound affection. God has such a special love for you that He has sent me

to give you a singularly outstanding vision and revelation." And
sure enough, Daniel was given such awesome heavenly visions that
he couldn't even stand up. The wonder of what he saw is exceeded
in Scripture only by the Revelation of Jesus Christ that was given
to the apostle John (the Book of Revelation).

So I find myself asking, "What did Daniel do to incur this kind
of affection from God? There's got to be a reason why God loved
him so much!" I figure if I could uncover why God loved Daniel so
much, then maybe I could give myself to that same kind of devotion.

I don't claim to understand the full reason why Daniel was
"greatly beloved" of God, but I do see one reason. To lay out that
one reason, I need to reproduce a passage from the fifth chapter of
the Book of Daniel.

Daniel 5

Daniel 5:1 Belshazzar the king made a great feast for a
thousand of his lords, and drank wine in the presence of
the thousand. 2 While he tasted the wine, Belshazzar
gave the command to bring the gold and silver vessels
which his father Nebuchadnezzar had taken from the
temple which had been in Jerusalem, that the king and
his lords, his wives, and his concubines might drink from
them. 3 Then they brought the gold vessels that had been
taken from the temple of the house of God which had
been in Jerusalem; and the king and his lords, his wives,
and his concubines drank from them. 4 They drank wine,
and praised the gods of gold and silver, bronze and iron,
wood and stone. 5 In the same hour the fingers of a man's
hand appeared and wrote opposite the lampstand on the
plaster of the wall of the king's palace; and the king saw
the part of the hand that wrote. 6 Then the king's countenance changed, and his thoughts troubled him, so that
the joints of his hips were loosened and his knees knocked
against each other. 7 The king cried aloud to bring in the
astrologers, the Chaldeans, and the soothsayers. The king
spoke, saying to the wise men of Babylon, "Whoever reads

this writing, and tells me its interpretation, shall be clothed with purple and have a chain of gold around his neck; and he shall be the third ruler in the kingdom." 8 Now all the king's wise men came, but they could not read the writing, or make known to the king its interpretation. 9 Then King Belshazzar was greatly troubled, his countenance was changed, and his lords were astonished. 10 The queen, because of the words of the king and his lords, came to the banquet hall. The queen spoke, saying, "O king, live forever! Do not let your thoughts trouble you, nor let your countenance change. 11 There is a man in your kingdom in whom is the Spirit of the Holy God. And in the days of your father, light and understanding and wisdom, like the wisdom of the gods, were found in him; and King Nebuchadnezzar your father—your father the king—made him chief of the magicians, astrologers, Chaldeans, and soothsayers. 12 Inasmuch as an excellent spirit, knowledge, understanding, interpreting dreams, solving riddles, and explaining enigmas were found in this Daniel, whom the king named Belteshazzar, now let Daniel be called, and he will give the interpretation." 13 Then Daniel was brought in before the king. The king spoke, and said to Daniel, "Are you that Daniel who is one of the captives from Judah, whom my father the king brought from Judah? 14 I have heard of you, that the Spirit of God is in you, and that light and understanding and excellent wisdom are found in you. 15 Now the wise men, the astrologers, have been brought in before me, that they should read this writing and make known to me its interpretation, but they could not give the interpretation of the thing. 16 And I have heard of you, that you can give interpretations and explain enigmas. Now if you can read the writing and make known to me its interpretation, you shall be clothed with purple and have a chain of gold around your neck, and shall be the third ruler in the kingdom." 17 Then Daniel answered, and said before the king, "Let your gifts be for yourself, and give your rewards to another; yet I will read the writing to the king, and make known to him the interpretation. 18 O king, the Most High God gave Nebuchadnezzar your father a kingdom and majesty, glory and honor. 19 And because of the majesty that He gave him, all peoples, nations, and languages trembled and feared before him. Whomever he wished, he executed; whomever he wished, he kept alive; whomever he wished, he set up; and whomever he wished, he put down. 20 But when his heart was lifted up, and his spirit was hardened in pride, he was deposed from his kingly throne, and they took his glory from him. 21 Then he was driven from the sons of men, his heart was made like the beasts, and his dwelling was with the wild donkeys. They fed him with grass like oxen, and his body was wet with the dew of heaven, till he knew that the Most High God rules in the kingdom of men, and appoints over it whomever He chooses. 22 But you his son, Belshazzar, have not humbled your heart, although you knew all this. 23 And you have lifted yourself up against the Lord of heaven. They have brought the vessels of His house before you, and you and your lords, your wives and your concubines, have drunk wine from them. And you have praised the gods of silver and gold, bronze and iron, wood and stone, which do not see or hear or know; and the God who holds your breath in His hand and owns all your ways, you have not glorified. 24 Then the fingers of the hand were sent from Him, and this writing was written. 25 And this is the inscription that was written: MENE, MENE, TEKEL, UPHARSIN. 26 This is the interpretation of each word. MENE: God has numbered your kingdom, and finished it; 27 TEKEL: You have been weighed in the balances, and found wanting; 28 PERES: Your kingdom has been divided, and given to the Medes and Persians." 29 Then Belshazzar gave the command, and they clothed Daniel with purple and put a chain of gold around his neck, and made a proclamation concerning him that he should be the third ruler in the kingdom.

Writing On The Wall

This passage describes a gala party in Babylon. While the wine is flowing, the food is bountiful, and the festivities are in full swing, suddenly a hand appears out of nowhere and writes something cryptic on the wall. Nobody in Belshazzar's kingdom is able to read and interpret the handwriting.

Then the Queen Mother enters the ballroom to speak to her son. She remembers how Daniel had interpreted the dreams of her late husband, king Nebuchadnezzar. So she says to the king, "You ought to find Daniel. He would be able to read and interpret the handwriting."

Belshazzar immediately fetches Daniel. Now, Daniel is not to be found in his former residence. At one time he had served as Nebuchadnezzar's right hand man and so would have lived near the king's palace. But when Belshazzar became king, he dismissed the cabinet members that had served his father and appointed his own cabinet. Daniel was ousted from his prestigious place of responsibility and influence at the king's right hand. Daniel 8:27 indicates that Daniel still worked for King Belshazzar, but it was in a much more menial and insignificant position. Daniel had been demoted, so they search to see where he now lives, and they find him.

Flattery And Praise

When they bring Daniel before Belshazzar, the first thing Belshazzar does is flatter him. Twice he says to Daniel, "I have heard of you" (verses 14 & 16). For a man who has been demoted to a menial job in some corner somewhere, these words of praise must have pulled at Daniel's ego. Imagine the President of the United States calling you into his Oval Office and saying to you, "I have heard of you." Now that would be impressive! Here is Belshazzar, the most powerful man in the world, acknowledging that Daniel's reputation has gone before him. "You're the talk of the king's court." That's very flattering indeed.

Then Belshazzar offers to reinstate Daniel to his former position, provided that he is able to read and interpret the handwriting on the wall.

Keep in mind that Daniel has been sent out to pasture. He's a discarded nobody. He's a semi-retired "has been" whom everyone has forgotten. And suddenly he faces an opportunity to regain honor, prestige, power, position, and wealth. All the other court members are drooling at the offer that has just been extended to him. What will Daniel say?

Daniel's response is most amazing. The flattery doesn't inflate his ego. The king's honor doesn't seduce him. The possibility of prestigious advancement doesn't make his heart race. Instead, he retorts to the king, "Let your gifts be for yourself, and give your rewards to another; yet I will read the writing to the king, and make known to him the interpretation" (verse 17). I want you to see that Daniel was completely unmoved by the king's compliments and honor. Far from tantalized, he is completely unimpressed with the honor that this mighty Monarch could bestow.

Living For God's Honor

If we could ask Daniel why the king's honor meant so little to him, I think he would tell us something like this: "Because there's only one thing I live for—the honor that God can bestow."

Daniel was a man who despised the honor that man could give because he valued the honor that God could give. And **this**, I believe, is one reason why God loved him so much. God is like, "Wow—this is incredible! I've got a man who values My honor so much that he repudiates the highest honors of man. I love this man! Here's a vessel that I can use."

I fully believe the reason the hand appeared and wrote on the wall, in the first place, was because God had a Daniel. If there had been no Daniel, there would have been no handwriting on the wall. God had a man who esteemed the honor of God over the honor of man, and so He was able to work in a most intriguing way to speak to the king of Babylon. **Where there's a Daniel—someone who lives for the honor of God—God is free to move in awesome ways.**

Warm Fuzzies

Has someone ever complimented you, and as a result you felt "warm fuzzies" on the inside? There is something in our sinfulness that is gratified when we receive commendation from people. "For men will praise you when you do well for yourself" (Psalm 49:18). So many people pursue this kind of praise—to be well esteemed in the sight of other people. Some are even driven by their need for the recognition of men.

This is an area in which the Spirit of God continues to challenge me most forcefully. The Spirit helped me to see that when I am nourished by the praises of man, it is actually idolatry. It's idolatry because I am finding life and sustenance in something other than Jesus. To be energized by the honor of man is to find fulfillment in something which Jesus despised.

Jesus' Perspective

Jesus expressed that disdain for man's praise when He said, "I do not receive honor from men" (John 5:41). He didn't merely say, "I don't go looking for the compliments of men," but He said, "When the compliments come, I don't even take them in to Myself."

Our Lord went on to say, "How can you believe, who receive honor from one another, and do not seek the honor that comes from the only God?" (John 5:44). It's as though Jesus were saying, "I don't understand you people. Why do you settle for something so paltry as the honor that man can give, when there is something so far greater available to you? The honor of man is so insignificant in contrast to the honor that your Heavenly Father is able to bestow." Jesus would testify, "There is no honor like My Father's honor."

"Looking unto Jesus, the author and finisher of our faith, who for the joy that was set before Him endured the cross, despising the shame" (Hebrews 12:2). The joy that was set before Him was this: the explosive, extravagant honor the Father would abundantly lavish upon Him in glory.

I can imagine the Father, sometime in the ages past, saying something like this to the Son: "Son, if You will embrace the suffering and death of the cross, it will please My heart greatly, and I will honor You."

And I can imagine the Son replying, "O holy Father, there are only two things I live for—to please You, and to receive Your honor. I would do anything for that!"

Jesus understood what it meant to be honored by the Father, and so it was for this that He lived and died. And did the Father honor Him? Oh my, how He honored Him! "Therefore God also has highly exalted Him and given Him the name which is above every name, that at the name of Jesus every knee should bow, of those in heaven, and of those on earth, and of those under the earth, and that every tongue should confess that Jesus Christ is Lord, to the glory of God the Father" (Philippians 2:9-11).

Seeking God's Glory

Jesus said, "He who speaks from himself seeks his own glory; but He who seeks the glory of the One who sent Him is true, and no unrighteousness is in Him" (John 7:18). I have been so convicted by this Scripture because Jesus is saying that every time I speak something that originates in my heart I am seeking my own glory. Every time I preach a sermon that has not gotten its impetus from the heart of the Father, I am speaking out of my own resources, and thus am seeking to look good before people. This verse has put an ardent desire in my heart to speak only that which the Spirit of God is giving me.

I am amazed at what Jesus says about the one who seeks the glory of the One who sent him. He said there is "no unrighteousness is in Him." In other words, **if I can get to the place where the only motivation that fills my heart is to bring honor and glory to God, then I will have arrived at a place of sinlessness.**

This business of desiring honor for ourselves—this is the final frontier. We think we're striving to glorify God until God shows us how much we look for glory ourselves. If only we could get to the place where there is no desire whatsoever within us to look good before men, and an exclusive and burning desire to see God glorified! Once we have perfected that attainment we will truly have entered into the grace of Christian perfection. For this we strain. Help us, Lord!

Summary

There are four great motivations, then, which we are seeking to cultivate and feed in our heart:

"I want to be with Him."
"I want to know Him."
"I want to please Him."
"I want His honor."

To be with Him, to know Him, to please Him, to receive His honor—for this I am desperate. By the grace of God, I will refrain from no measure, I will spare no expense, I will embrace any discipline, I will travel any distance, I will be still as long as it takes, I will hazard any hardship, I will chance whatever reproach, misunderstanding, or rejection it might involve, to pursue these four things. I must gain Christ!

Section Four

FRIENDSHIP WITH GOD

11

THREE STAGES
OF CONSECRATION

"Greater love has no one than this, than to lay down one's
life for his friends. You are My friends if you do whatever I command you. No longer do I call you servants,
for a servant does not know what his master is doing; but
I have called you friends, for all things that I heard from
My Father I have made known to you" (John 15:13-15).

In this deeply stirring passage, Jesus differentiates between a
servant and a friend. Jesus indicates that at one time His disciples
were merely servants, but through relationship-building time together the disciples had come to be Jesus' friends.

This places a great goal before us. "Lord, I don't want to be
Your servant only; I want to progress to the level of friendship."

There are different levels of relationship with Christ. We grow
in our love relationship with Him, from glory to glory. I want to
cite some passages that point to three general levels of Christian
consecration or maturity. Although using different terminology,
these passages point to the same dynamic—how we grow in grace,
ever moving toward the fullness of Christ. The first such passage
is John 15:13-15, which is quoted above.

First Level: Believer

The first level of Christian experience is what I will call "a believer." We all start off as believers. When we're first born into the family of God, we all believe that Jesus is the Son of God and the Savior of the world. We have repented, believed, confessed, been baptized in water, and our names are written in the Lamb's Book of Life.

Many people believe and accept Christ as their Savior, but they hesitate to make Him the Lord of their life. In many ways they still want to live for themselves. They have a place in the kingdom of God, but they are very immature.

It's one thing to be a believer; it's another thing to become a servant of Christ.

Second Level: Servant

What does it mean to be a servant of God? A servant is someone who has completely surrendered himself to obeying Jesus. He has fully embraced the cross, has knelt at the altar of consecration, and now is committed to 100% radical obedience.

A servant has given himself entirely to God. His time, his talents, his treasures—everything is fully submitted to the Lordship of Jesus Christ. He can say along with Paul, "I am a bondslave of Jesus Christ."

Servanthood is a glorious kingdom attainment! It is a wonderful day when we finally realize that we'll never be satisfied with anything less than absolute surrender. Although we still struggle with the flesh, the heart commitment is there. We want to be fully available to God.

Third Level: Friendship.

This is the ultimate dimension of Christian living. There is a realm in God where Jesus is not only **my** Friend, but I am also **His** friend. **At the servant dimension I come to enjoy Jesus as my Friend; at the friendship level I become the kind of friend that He enjoys**.

Before we look more closely at the differences between a servant and a friend, let me point to two other passages that also describe the Christian walk in three general spheres of experience.

30-, 60-, And 100-Fold

Jesus divided the fruitfulness of the Christian life into three general spheres when He said, "'But others fell on good ground and yielded a crop: some a hundredfold, some sixty, some thirty'" (Matthew 13:8). In context, Jesus is talking about the comparative yield of different kinds of good soil. Some soil will produce a 30-fold harvest, some will produce 60-fold, and some 100-fold.

Jesus is pointing to the fact that Christians have different levels of fruitfulness in the kingdom. Some are simply more effective in the Lord's harvest than others.

The 30-fold sphere describes those who bear a harvest as much as thirty percent; the 60-fold sphere describes those who bear a harvest from thirty to sixty percent; the 100-fold sphere describes those who bear a harvest from sixty to one hundred percent. In other words, each sphere represents a continuum, and so a believer may find himself in a constant state of flux as he grows and matures into ever greater fruitfulness.

These three spheres of fruitfulness coincide with Jesus' later teaching in John 15 on servants and friends in this way:

30-fold coincides with "believer"
60-fold coincides with "servant"
100-fold coincides with "friend"

At first glance it may appear that I'm trying to force a connection here, but I believe you'll find this application to bear up under scrutiny. The most identifiable quality of a "friend of God" is fruitfulness, which coincides with the 100-fold harvest. The unifying factor in all of this is fruitfulness.

A "believer" operates in the sphere of one to thirty percent fruitfulness. He has an impact on other people's lives, but his witness is rendered less than fully effective because of the immaturity and compromise in his life.

A "servant" moves into greater fruitfulness, as much as 60-fold, because he has embraced the discipline of Romans 12:1, and his life is now "a living sacrifice" to God. There is so much grace to explore in this dimension, and so Jesus describes it as a sphere that ranges from thirty to sixty percent fruitfulness.

A "friend" moves into the ultimate dimension of fruitfulness, where he learns to move ever closer to the ultimate attainment: 100-fold fruitfulness.

Turn to the next chapter and we'll look at another matching passage.

12

LITTLE CHILDREN, YOUNG MEN, FATHERS

I want to cite one final passage which points to three general levels of Christian living:

> I write to you, little children, because your sins are forgiven you for His name's sake. I write to you, fathers, because you have known Him who is from the beginning. I write to you, young men, because you have overcome the wicked one. I write to you, little children, because you have known the Father. I have written to you, fathers, because you have known Him who is from the beginning. I have written to you, young men, because you are strong, and the word of God abides in you, and you have overcome the wicked one (1 John 2:12-14).

The apostle John divides the Christian life into three general spheres of spiritual maturity: little children, young men, and fathers. These three terms are parallel concepts with the other two passages cited in the previous chapter.

Little Children

The "little children" are young "believers" who, because of their immaturity, are not really productive in the kingdom. That's one of the characteristics of children. Kids are an absolute delight because they fill a home with joy, warmth, and fun, but they don't bring much income into the home. In fact, not only are babies totally non-productive, they are incredibly demanding. They seem to "take" more than they can "give."

Young believers are often the same way. Instead of producing a great kingdom harvest, they often seem to require a lot of time and energy.

But this is normal. It's normal for everyone to start off as a baby in Christ. It's just not normal to stay a baby. God wants us to grow up.

Young Men

The "young men" are "servants" who have come into a greater dimension of kingdom productivity, as much as 60-fold fruitfulness. These young men are strong in grace, they're able to teach the word of God, and they've learned how to resist and overcome the devil in spiritual warfare. Because of these attainments, they touch other people in a greater way than when they were "little children."

Little children will become young men if they are nourished properly and allowed to grow. But sadly enough, many people seem to remain "spiritual children" for many years. Some believers have been with Christ for years, but they still don't know how to overcome the enemy or how to instruct others in the truths of the faith.

Little children look at the attainments of young men and think to themselves, "That must be the ultimate dimension in Christ! To come to a place where every known sin has been brought into subjection and where Jesus is crowned Lord of every area—wow! When I get to that place I will have arrived!" But there's more to attain than just the place of the "young men," far more.

Fathers

Spiritual "fathers" are those who have come to know God and as a result are truly "friends" with Christ. They have entered the greatest dimensions of fruitfulness in the kingdom, even approaching 100-fold fruitfulness. The foremost quality of spiritual fathers is that they are reproducers of spiritual children. Again, the issue of maturity (fatherhood) is fruitfulness. Fathers beget children.

Paul distinguishes between 60-fold young men and 100-fold fathers in this way: "For though you might have ten thousand instructors in Christ, yet you do not have many fathers; for in Christ Jesus I have begotten you through the gospel" (1 Corinthians 4:15). The "instructors" correspond to the "young men" who are strong in the word and able to teach. There are many young men but not many fathers. With each level of maturity the numbers decrease.

Following is a simple diagram which shows the parallel nature of the passages we have just discussed and the three general levels of Christian maturity.

	1 John 2:12-14	Matthew 13:8	John 15:13-15
sonship:	"little children"	30-fold	believer
discipleship:	"young men"	60-fold	"servant"
partnership:	"fathers"	100-fold	"friend"

The "little children" are paralleled with "sonship" because these have become sons of God. The "young men" are paralleled with "discipleship" because they have embraced the cross and become true disciples of Christ. The "fathers" are paralleled with "partnership" because they have learned the secret of becoming yoked with Christ and working together with Him.

We'll discuss this diagram further in the next chapter.

13

PARTNERSHIP WITH GOD

Last chapter we introduced the following diagram:

	1 John 2:12-14	Matthew 13:8	John 15:13-15
sonship:	"little children"	30-fold	believer
discipleship:	"young men"	60-fold	"servant"
partnership:	"fathers"	100-fold	"friend"

Issues Of Maturity

This diagram helps us to see some interesting dynamics regarding spiritual maturity.

Perhaps you've wondered if there's any way to determine someone's spiritual maturity level. The issue in maturity is **fruitfulness**. The immature are not so fruitful; the mature are more fruitful. Maturity in Christ is not necessarily linked to how long one has known the Lord or how active one has been in ministry. Maturity has nothing to do with position or title; there are many immature leaders in the church. Jesus isn't impressed with human accomplishments or educational degrees. He's looking for vines that will bear much fruit.

I used to equate maturity with stability. If someone was real stable in God then I thought they were very mature. But now I see that maturity has less to do with status and more to do with function. Sometimes I've heard saints say things like, "I carried that ministry for fifteen years, now it's somebody else's turn." In this way, some saints actually decrease in fruitfulness as they get older. This is quite sad because God has so much more for them.

God intends for 30-fold Christians to become 60-fold Christians. I did not always understand this. I used to think that we're stuck at one of these levels. "Once a 30-folder, always a 30-folder" is how I used to think. I see now that I had confused fruitfulness with stewardship of talents. Let me explain the difference I now see between talents and fruitfulness.

A talent is a God-given gifting over which we have no determination. In other words, we don't decide our areas of gifting, God does. He gives us talents in specific areas and then holds us responsible to cultivate and develop those talents and abilities. When it comes to talents, you've got what you've got. For example, some people are gifted musically and they learn to make music with comparatively little effort. There are others who are less gifted musically, however, and can spend years in music lessons with relatively little progress. Our level of attainment in any area will always be limited by the degree of giftedness God has given us in that area.

Fruitfulness, on the other hand, has to do with how productive we become in our areas of talent and gifting. When it comes to fruitfulness, we can always improve. We can't change our level of gifting, but we can improve how effectively we function in that gifting. If I am a 2-talent person I cannot decide to become a 3-talent person, but I can purpose, in God's grace, to become the most fruitful 2-talent person I can possibly be. God designs for all believers to progress all the way to 100-fold fruitfulness. Not many achieve that place, but it's available to all. Regardless of your level of gifting, God wants you to exercise your giftings at 100-fold fruitfulness.

Each level of maturity has a certain threshold which is difficult to cross. To cross the threshold from being a child to becoming a young man in God requires the wholehearted embracing of the cross, dying to self, and living only to God. To cross the threshold from being a young man to a spiritual father is an even more painful transition. Young men have learned how to exercise their talents for God, but to become spiritual fathers they must learn another dimension of dependence upon the Spirit of God.

Moving Into Fatherhood

Let me talk a little more about this transition. 60-fold "young men" are hard workers. They have learned to labor in the vineyard, and they are usually easy to spot because they are very active. They are busy for God. As they take on more and more areas of ministry responsibility, they become more and more stretched. Finally, they come to the place where they feel totally maxed out. "If someone gives me one more ball to juggle," they think, "I'll probably drop everything!"

And just about this time, a father in the faith strolls by. This young man watches him in total amazement. The spiritual father is so much more relaxed, he's not even breaking a sweat, but he is so much more fruitful in the kingdom. (Fathers have learned that fruitfulness is not linked to one's level of activity.) The young man is simultaneously amazed and perplexed because he can't understand how this father can produce so much kingdom fruit with seemingly so little effort.

As for himself, this young man is running full tilt. He is serving Jesus with his entire being, but he cannot possibly add one more thing to his schedule. He knows there are greater dimensions of fruitfulness in God, but he has no idea how to access them. He begins to feel dissatified with his place in God because he has reached 60-fold fruitfulness and cannot seem to get beyond it. A cry for more of Christ begins to arise from deep within his heart.

The Lord knows that this young man will not be able to enter the highest dimensions of consecration without help. So God says, "Let me do you a favor." And He goes—WHACK! He wounds the young man. This is how God introduces the 60-fold Christian to the dimension of 100-fold fruitfulness. It's summarized in one word: pruning. **God takes the 60-fold young man who is full of energy and vision and cuts him back to nothing**. Through the trauma of the pruning process, the 60-fold servant begins to learn to tap into a lifesource that is greater than his talents and energies. The Spirit trains him to walk in a different dimension in the Spirit which will actually slow him down and make him more fruitful.

Partnership

I would like to share with you a personal way in which the Lord has challenged me to move from discipleship toward partnership with Him.

For several years now I have been seeking the Lord most fervently for a physical healing. As I have prayed about this, the Spirit enabled me to see that I need to reorient how I relate to the Father. The Lord wants me to mature in the way I approach Him in prayer.

In the past, I have approached prayer as the means of getting from God what I want (which in my case was a healing). I imagined it working something like this: if I responded properly to all His dealings and had the right kind of faith, God would then be able to heal me. I saw it like the pins of a lock—once all the pins of the lock were properly engaged, the lock would snap open, and I would be healed. So the key to divine healing, in my mind, was getting everything right all at once.

But there are a couple things wrong with this picture. First, it paints the Father as a somewhat reluctant giver who will not dispense grace until everything is in order. But if God's grace were given to me only when I responded correctly, I would never have any grace on my life! Second, this skewed picture suggests that my job is to "jump through heaven's hoops" so that I can extract from heaven what I want.

The Lord has "called me higher" to relate to Him on a different level altogether. Instead of my simply being the supplicant and His being the supplier, the Lord wants me to come to a "workers together" mentality (1 Corinthians 3:9). I am to share His heart so completely that His desires become my desires, His plans become my plans, and His work becomes my work. **He wants me to be His partner, someone who so fully shares the pulsations of His heart that my life becomes an extension of His will and purpose on the earth**. When I truly learn to partner with Christ, it will still be true that it's God's will to heal me, but I may find my healing coming in a way I had not personally anticipated.

The fully mature partner of the Lord Jesus moves in parallel motion with heaven. He waits upon God until he perceives the heart of the Father, and then he works on earth in the power of the Spirit to be a catalyst for God's purposes to be accomplished here in time and space. Rather than trying to extract his agenda from God, he is now learning to be a cooperative enforcer of God's agenda on earth.

This dimension of life in the Spirit is called "friendship with God."

14

A SERVANT, OR A FRIEND?

Friendship With God

> "Greater love has no one than this, than to lay down one's life for his friends. You are My friends if you do whatever I command you. No longer do I call you servants, for a servant does not know what his master is doing; but I have called you friends, for all things that I heard from My Father I have made known to you" (John 15:13-15).

I have been in full-time ministry for over fifteen years, and have been, to the best of my ability, a faithful servant of Jesus. I have worked hard for Him, have watched His blessings attend my life, and have had the joy of furthering His kingdom. But I am seeing that there is a level of relationship with Jesus that is higher than servanthood, and it is that of friendship. O to be a friend of God!

Based upon these words of Jesus in John 15, I would like to suggest some distinctions between a servant and a friend.

Servant Or Friend?

1. Servanthood is a great attainment, but it is not the highest attainment in Christ.

Great joy fills the heart when one finally lays his life completely at the feet of Jesus and says, "I'm Yours, Lord. I will serve You with all my heart and soul. Whatever You ask of me I will do." There are many "believers," but not as many "servants." And there are fewer still "friends" of God.

2. A servant is like an employee; a friend is brought into management and made a co-owner.

3. A servant can be deployed anywhere where there's a need; the Master has many menial tasks that need to be done. But a friend is allowed to work in those areas that are most significant in the eyes of the Master.

4. A friend prays differently from a servant.

A servant desires to move the hand of God; a friend desires to know the heart of God. Servants are just trying to get the job done, so they plead with heaven to help them. "Bless my labors, Lord!" the servant cries. But a friend asks, "Lord, what are **You** doing? What are **You** thinking?" A servant wants the Lord to hear him; a friend wants to hear from the Lord.

A friend won't harangue God with his own requests but will hold his tongue until he knows the mind of the Spirit. A servant prays for the blessings he desires, but a friend seeks to be an intercessor through whom heaven's will can come to earth.

The Lord is calling us beyond what has been commonly referred to as "prevailing prayer." It is certainly a valid form of prayer, but it is not the highest form of prayer. The term "prevailing prayer" carries the idea that my task in prayer is to convince God to supply what I want. Better yet, the Lord is calling us to "cooperative prayer." In cooperative prayer, I become the vehicle on earth to birth through intercession the perfect will of God in heaven.

5. A servant measures things by results, whereas a friend evaluates things according to the Master's pleasure.

It's possible to obtain results in kingdom pursuits but not have the Master's full blessing. Someone once said of a certain prominent ministry, "You can't knock it, they get results." But results are not the means of measuring the eternal value of our ministries. Jesus said there would be many servants with significant results who would not inherit the kingdom because they didn't have a relationship with their Lord (Matthew 7:22). In calling Him "Lord, Lord," they were claiming to be His servants. But He said to them, "I never knew you."

Above all, a friend longs for the smile of Jesus upon what he's doing. Whether others think his accomplishments are significant is irrelevant. His only desire is to do those things that elicit the nodding approval of the Lord Jesus.

6. The issue for a servant is faithfulness (Matthew 25:21); the issue for a friend is love (John 15:13).

Martha and Mary were two sisters who loved Jesus dearly, but they expressed their love quite differently. Martha showed her love by serving Jesus faithfully; Mary showed her love by sitting at Jesus' feet and hanging on His every word. Jesus commended Mary as having "chosen that good part, which will not be taken away from her" (Luke 10:42). As long as she busied herself with faithful service, Martha would stay at the servant dimension. Mary, however, had a passion to become the friend of Jesus.

A servant is willing to work for the Master, but a friend wants to be with the Master.

7. It's a more demanding commitment to be a friend than a servant.

Any friendship requires investment of time and energy. In one sense it's easier to keep our relationship with Jesus at the Master/servant level because friendship requires more focused energy and larger blocks of time commitment. But the Master/servant level will never be as rewarding or fulfilling.

The friend and the servant both work for the Master, but after the work is done the servant is dismissed whereas the friend sits down with the Master.

8. The most gripping distinction of all is made by Jesus Himself in this passage. Jesus said that a servant just does what he's told without necessarily understanding why he's doing what he's doing. But a friend is confided in.

Jesus said, "I have called you friends, for all things that I heard from My Father I have made known to you." Jesus is saying, "The fact that I have disclosed to you all things that the Father has spoken to me is the indicator that you have become My friends." Jesus treats His friends differently; He confides in them.

A friend is told the thoughts and intentions behind the plan of action. A servant is told what to do, but a friend is told why. To say it precisely, Jesus confides His **purposes** to His friends.

15

OBEDIENCE TO HIS PURPOSES

Vision Versus Purpose

I have been a man of vision. I have established goals for myself each year and have urged the leaders in our church to do likewise. Most books on Christian leadership deal to one degree or another with the necessity of establishing vision, setting goals, and learning how to evaluate the progress toward those goals.

We adopt a vision for our ministry for this year, and for the next five years, and for the next ten years. We develop a Vision Statement or a Mission Statement. We brainstorm what exploits we might accomplish for God's kingdom. We are visionary leaders.

With only one slight problem: God doesn't operate out of vision. He doesn't have a vision for your life or for your ministry, and He doesn't have a vision for this planet. God only has **purpose**. He has a purpose for your life and for the entire human race, and **His purposes will be accomplished**.

As I speak of "vision" in this sense, I am speaking of that forward-looking hope of future progress. Vision is hopeful; purpose is as good as done. God does not merely "hope" that His plans will be fulfilled, for He has determined in advance that they will be accomplished. Now, God does impart vision to us (Habakkuk 2:2), but it is always in conformity with His purpose. In other words, a true vision from God is certain to be fulfilled because it is the purpose of God revealed in advance.

Much of the time, when we think we're operating out of godly vision, we're merely working in human creativity. This is evidenced by the sheer volume of goals that we've never achieved.

We're reduced to being visionary when we don't know God's purposes. After getting a general sense of the game plan, servants develop a vision of what they can do for God; a friend, on the other hand, is God's confidant who hears His heart and perceives His purpose for his life and ministry.

Creativity And Obedience

God doesn't ask us to be creative but to be obedient. Sometimes the creativity of Christian leaders does damage to the kingdom of God because we mobilize believers in efforts that didn't originate in the heart of God. Our good ideas can actually restrict our ability to share in God's purposes. The way of God is this: "Wait on Me **until**—until I speak to you."

I've discovered that it's much easier to be creative than obedient because creativity requires planning, but obedience requires listening. It's easier to plan than to listen. It's easier to press ahead with my own thoughts than to wait upon God for His thoughts.

And when you're waiting on God, there's no telling when He's going to come to you. You might wait for days, weeks, months, or even years. I said, "Lord, I can come up with ten creative ideas before You even say anything!" That's where the real test is, however, because when we finally hear from God His ideas are always worth the wait. Just one solitary thought of God's is many times more effective than our most brilliant profusion of ideas.

This is good news for those who have never felt exceptionally creative in terms of natural gifting. Some of us have felt inferior when we've stood next to someone with a multitude of talents. But if we're all called to be obedient rather than creative, can you understand how this puts us all at the same level? The naturally creative person has no advantage over the one who feels like a creative dullard. We're all reduced to this one common denominator: we must hear from God. There is great liberty here for those who will receive it.

A servant operates in the vision of what could be; a friend operates in the confidence of what will be. A friend of God will accomplish far more, for he will not muddy the waters with his own creative juices. Instead of getting in God's way, he will get in God's ways.

The Ways of God

Here's the amazing part: when you begin to hear God's ideas and to act upon them, others will be astounded at your "creativity." The reason is simply because God's thoughts and ways are so different from ours that when He begins to reveal His purposes to us they will be strikingly extraordinary.

> "For My thoughts are not your thoughts, nor are your ways My ways," says the LORD. "For as the heavens are higher than the earth, so are My ways higher than your ways, and My thoughts than your thoughts" (Isaiah 55:8-9).

If an idea smells and looks and feels like something you'd come up with, then be assured—it's infinitely different from God's way. God's way of thinking is not only in a different ballpark, it's on a different planet.

One way to know it's God's idea is that you would have never come up with that idea on your own.

God's ways will always be different from your ways. You can get frustrated with that, or you can choose to be attracted by that. (God made us to be naturally attracted to that which is different from ourselves.) Let's choose to be fascinated by His ways. The fact that we do not understand His ways should fuel our desire to know Him better.

Beyond Imagination

Paul writes in Ephesians 3:20, "Now to Him who is able to do exceedingly abundantly above all that we ask or think, according to the power that works in us." There is a power at work in me that far exceeds my thinking. There is a power at work in me that far exceeds my imagination. So why limit what God wants to do in and through my life to the smallness of my own creative thinking?

By God's grace I'm dispensing with this business of spending time dreaming up innovative ways to do the work of the kingdom, with pen and notepad in hand, imagining what I might be able to do for God. Instead, I'm going to give myself to ardent listening—with a pen and notepad in hand—noting those promptings and directives that come from the heart of God. Have done with our own ingenuity, let's tune into what **He** wants to do by His incredible power which resides in and flows through us!

Paul continues, "to Him be glory in the church by Christ Jesus to all generations, forever and ever. Amen" (Ephesians 3:21). My ideas have a way of directing a certain percentage of attention to myself; His ideas redound only to His glory. That makes His ideas not only better, but safe.

16

BECOMING HIS FRIEND

Do not say, "I am God's friend." You can say, "God is my Friend" because that would be true, but it is presumptuous to call yourself a friend of God. That is for God to decide. He says who His friends are. Thus, you never see anyone in Scripture claiming to be God's friend. Abraham did not call himself a friend of God, it was God who said that Abraham was His friend.

Abraham

Abraham was called the friend of God (James 2:23). He wasn't a man of vision; he was a man to whom God chose to reveal His purposes. God determined that he could confide in Abraham. This is seen so clearly in the following passage.

Genesis 18:17 And the LORD said, "Shall I hide from Abraham what I am doing, 18 since Abraham shall surely become a great and mighty nation, and all the nations of the earth shall be blessed in him? 19 For I have known him, in order that he may command his children and his household after him, that they keep the way of the LORD, to do righteousness and justice, that the LORD may bring to Abraham what He has spoken to him." 20 And the LORD said, "Because the outcry against Sodom and

Gomorrah is great, and because their sin is very grave, 21
I will go down now and see whether they have done altogether according to the outcry against it that has come to
Me; and if not, I will know." 22 Then the men turned
away from there and went toward Sodom, but Abraham
still stood before the LORD.

Notice two qualities of spiritual fatherhood (friendship with
God) in this passage: God chose to confide His purposes to
Abraham; and God said, "For I have known him." Abraham knew
God and God knew him.

As Abraham grew in his knowledge of God and God's purposes, he eventually came to the place where he was able to pass
the ultimate test of friendship. God needed someone who would
prophetically demonstrate many centuries beforehand the eventual
death and resurrection of His Son. It's as though God said, "I need
someone who will be so surrendered to My purposes that he will
obey Me even to the point of raising a knife over his only son. In so
doing, he will be an object lesson to show how I will kill My only
begotten Son. This would require a very extraordinary man, a man
who has come into true spiritual fatherhood. If such a man were to
be found, He would truly be My friend."

When God finally made this ultimate request of Abraham,
Abraham didn't pause for a moment but immediately rose up and
took his son on the three-day journey to the place where he would
offer Isaac as a sacrifice to God. When God saw Abraham's implicit obedience He said, "Now, **here** is a friend of Mine!"

All of us owe our relationship with God to the fact that long
ago a man (Abraham) became God's friend. Abraham is our spiritual father, and we are his spiritual inheritance. God has a great
heritage reserved for His friends.

When you look at the amazing promises that God gave to
Abraham, you realize that Abraham did nothing to incur them. All
he did was obey God and believe what God told him. But God
enjoyed Abraham so much that He singled him out for great blessing. There is a great posterity for God's friends.

The Pathway To Friendship

Someone might ask, "How can I become a friend of God?"
The answer is important because you don't just decide you're going to become somebody's best friend. Friendship is something

that must "click." There must be a compatibility of personality, of interests, a certain "chemistry" that makes a friendship a mutually meaningful relationship. God isn't the friend of some of us because He simply can't relate to us. He knows we love Him, but we're so self-absorbed that we keep ourselves at the servant level.

Jesus made it clear that the pathway to friendship is through implicit obedience. He said, "You are My friends if you do whatever I command you" (John 15:14). He was saying, "As you give yourself to radical obedience, the pathway to friendship with God will open before you."

The test of friendship is, will you wait until God tells you what to do? When servants aren't hearing a clear directive from God, they use their best judgment and select a course of action. (May the Lord help us to learn that our judgment is never best.) Servants live by the popular idiom, "You can't steer a stationary vehicle," so they figure they need to step out and just do something. **A friend, however, waits until he hears from God. His consuming passion is to hear and obey**.

Sometimes circumstances scream for immediate action—and there's no word from God. "It's midnight, Lord! I have to make a decision!" God says nothing. "Lord, now it's **past** midnight! What do You want me to do?" Sometimes God waits past midnight because the discipline of waiting for the Master's directive is vital to becoming His friend. This is the fiery test of the **servant** of God. If he will wait—even past the deadline if need be—he will learn something about **friendship** with God.

We don't decide to become God's friend; God invites us upward to that dimension of relationship. This is the principle of Luke 14:10: "But when you are invited, go and sit down in the lowest place, so that when he who invited you comes he may say to you, '**Friend, go up higher**.' Then you will have glory in the presence of those who sit at the table with you." It's an awesome thing when God calls us up higher to the place of friendship with Him.

Until then, all we can do is give ourselves to 100% obedience and ask Him to draw us higher. Ultimately, friendship with God is not something we can contrive or manage. We are drawn into friendship by the compelling overtures of the Holy Spirit. As the Holy Spirit reveals to us what it means to be a friend of the Almighty

God of the universe, a prayer begins to arise in our hearts, "Lord, plant my feet on higher ground." You cannot plant yourself on higher ground; you can only cry for Him to draw you. He places the cry in your heart and He draws you—from beginning to end it is all of Him.

Joshua

Joshua is a great example of a servant who longed to become a friend. This is seen clearly in this verse:

> "So the LORD spoke to Moses face to face, as a man speaks to his friend. And he would return to the camp, but his servant Joshua the son of Nun, a young man, did not depart from the tabernacle" (Exodus 33:11).

Here Moses is rightly called the friend of God. He had come into the highest dimensions of intimacy with God, "face to face." And Joshua is rightly called the servant.

Joshua saw Moses' friendship with God, and he yearned to have the same kind of relationship with God. But he realized he had as yet only attained servanthood. He was a young servant of God with lots of vision and energy, but as he watched Moses he knew there was more.

So what did Joshua do? Did he just shrug and say, "Well, no sense in killing myself here, either God chooses you or He doesn't"? No. Joshua pressed into God for himself. Even after Moses would return to the camp, Joshua "did not depart from the tabernacle." This is the John 15 invitation of Jesus, "Abide in Me."

In the final analysis, the chief preoccupation of friends is simply this: to delight in each other.

Marks Of Friendship

I want to point to three other qualities that interestingly enough characterize friends of God.

> And He said to them, "Can you make the friends of the bridegroom fast while the bridegroom is with them? But

the days will come when the bridegroom will be taken away from them; then they will fast in those days" (Luke 5:34-35).

1. Friends fast. Fasting is the domain of those who have come into true friendship with Jesus.

> "And I say to you, My friends, do not be afraid of those who kill the body, and after that have no more that they can do. But I will show you whom you should fear: fear Him who, after He has killed, has power to cast into hell; yes, I say to you, fear Him!" (Luke 12:4-5).

2. Friends fear. Jesus is saying, "My friends, fear Me!" Although friends have come into wonderful intimacy with God, they have not adopted a casual, chummy, or flippant attitude toward Him. To the contrary, because they have come to know Him they fear Him more than ever.

> A friend loves at all times, and a brother is born for adversity (Proverbs 17:17).

3. A friend always loves. A friend of God loves God even in the toughest of times. This is the litmus test of friendship with God: do I still love Him even when He allows inexplicable trauma to hit my life?

17

THE BRIDEGROOM'S FRIEND

Our study on friendship with God would not be complete without looking at the man who is called the friend of Jesus. Read again these words of John the Baptist:

> "He who has the bride is the bridegroom; but the friend of the bridegroom, who stands and hears him, rejoices greatly because of the bridegroom's voice. Therefore this joy of mine is fulfilled. He must increase, but I must decrease" (John 3:29-30).

John had been preaching and baptizing for some time, and Jesus was just new on the scene. Crowds were starting to gather around Jesus, and so John's followers asked his opinion of Jesus. This was John's response as he described his relationship to Jesus. John likened Jesus to a "bridegroom" and himself to the "friend of the bridegroom." Thus, in an indirect way he called himself the friend of Jesus.

Perhaps the following diagram of John 3:29 will help us understand this verse better.

3 characters:	John 3:29 Then:	Now:
Bridegroom	Jesus	Jesus
Bride	People of Israel	Church
Friend of groom	John the Baptist	Leaders

Explanation Of Diagram

John the Baptist paints a word picture by using three characters: a bride, a bridegroom, and the friend of the bridegroom. In his day, John was speaking specifically of Jesus as the bridegroom, the Jews as the bride, and he referred to himself as the friend of the bridegroom. The verse has an application for us today as well, however. In its contemporary application Jesus is still the bridegroom, but the bride takes on the fuller meaning of the Church, and the friend of the bridegroom represents leaders in the body of Christ who are called of God to prepare the Church for Christ's return.

Even as John prepared the people for Christ's **first** coming, God is wanting to raise up true friends of Jesus today who will prepare the people for His **second** coming.

Wedding Symbolism

This word picture of an impending wedding that John the Baptist paints is filled with meaning and carries some very instructional principles for us.

Principle #1: The bridegroom "has the bride."

In other words, the groom possesses her heart. Jesus has the affections of the Church. Through His sacrificial death, He has won her love, her heart, her sole devotion. She only has eyes for Him. He is the rightful owner of her every affection. It is only proper that she be completely and totally preoccupied with thoughts of and desires for Him.

Principle #2: The role of the friend is to serve the bride until the bridegroom arrives.

The friend of the bridegroom, in contemporary vernacular, would be called "the best man." As the bridegroom's best friend, it's his job to help the groom with wedding preparations.

Since the Bridegroom (Jesus) is away, the friend (a church leader) finds himself at the side of the Bride (the Church), helping her as the wedding day approaches. The friend serves her, helps her, protects her, and prepares her for the big day.

Principle #3: The friend nurtures and feeds the bride's affections for the bridegroom.

The Bride of Christ has a problem: the Bridegroom has ascended to heaven and left her here on earth. And the longer the Bridegroom delays His coming, the more the Bride becomes distracted with other interests.

She begins to say to the friend, "I know He is wonderful, and I love Him, I really do. But I remember a time when I was **really** in love with Him. At one point I would have given up **anything** for Him, but now that He's been gone so long, I'm not so sure. I mean, look at this neat thing over here. Is He really worth my saying 'no' to these other attractions?"

The Bridegroom's friend has something to say to her. The reason he's the Groom's friend in the first place is because he has recognized the greatness of the Groom. He knows the beauty and splendor of the Bridegroom, and in fact he delights in the Groom himself. So the friend is able to praise the Groom's beauty to the Bride.

The friend says, "Listen, don't look at those other loves. They're trash. I'm telling you, you're the luckiest girl in town. You've got the best! He's the pick of the crop. You've landed the biggest fish in the whole ocean. There is no one else like Him! All the other virgins are jealous because you've got the affections of the most handsome guy around. He has chosen you. Believe me, you don't want to dump Him for some cheap substitute. Save yourself! Keep yourself pure and chaste, exclusively for Him!"

So the friend reminds her of the Bridegroom's beauty. He talks of His fiery eyes, His shining face, the delightful words of His mouth, and how much He loves her. And she says, "Yes, yes! You're right! How could I have almost forgotten? He is beautiful beyond description; He is the lover of my soul. I must keep myself only for Him!"

In this way he is serving as a true friend of the Bridegroom.

The issue for the Bride is this: Will she keep her love pure and wholly devoted to the Bridegroom for the duration that His coming is delayed?

Principle #4: A friend must guard his heart because of the beauty of the bride.

The friend's temptation, while the Bridegroom is away, is to flirt with the Bride. She is ripe with passions and affections, and she can be taken advantage of right now. She is incredibly beautiful, she has a lot to give, and he could exploit the Bridegroom's absence by courting the Bride's affections.

While he is serving her, it is only proper that the Bride render due honor to the Groom's friend. But she ought not share the affections she has bottled up and reserving for the Bridegroom—not even with His friend.

If the Groom's friend is a **true** friend, he will flee any opportunity to gain the affections of the Bride, but instead will protect and reserve her affections for the Bridegroom.

The friend here represents church leaders who are called by Christ to serve His Bride. Many pastors and leaders have allowed the Bride to place improper affections upon them. Not only have they allowed it, they've enjoyed it. I can speak candidly here because I am the first of offenders.

Leaders, if we are true friends of Christ, we will conduct ourselves in such a way that the bride is not taken by our own abilities but rather is enthralled more and more with the beauty of Christ's face.

Principle #5: A friend decreases.

John said, "For He must increase, but I must decrease" (John 3:30). John was prepared to decrease, but even so it was a painful thing. John discovered that once Jesus showed up, people weren't so interested in hearing John's message anymore.

Before the Bridegroom comes back, the friend is laying his life down for the Bride. He's serving, giving, helping, protecting, encouraging, guiding, and sacrificing for the Bride—all because the Bridegroom is his Friend. But everything changes when the Bridegroom returns. Suddenly, the friend is completely forgotten by the Bride. Her Lover is back, and the friend doesn't even enter her thoughts.

At this point, it would be tempting for the friend to feel somewhat abandoned. I can suppose him griping to the Bridegroom, "Hey, while You were gone, I did everything for You; and now that You've arrived, it's as though I don't exist." And he's right. The Bride has quite forgotten him. It's because the friend doesn't have the Bride, the Groom does.

The **true** friend of the Groom, however, is glad to decrease. The friend's fulfillment comes in seeing the undistracted delight in the eyes of the Bride and Groom as they enjoy their reunion one with the other. John the Baptist was a true friend to Jesus, for he said, "The friend of the bridegroom, who stands and hears him, rejoices greatly because of the bridegroom's voice. Therefore this joy of mine is fulfilled."

John is saying, "Before the Bridegroom showed up, I was the focus of attention among the people. Now that He has appeared, He is getting more and more attention by the people and my crowds are getting smaller and smaller. And I'm rejoicing about this! The fact that my popularity is dwindling and His is increasing fulfills my joy."

May the Lord raise up many such friends of the Bridegroom in this hour, who will be useful vessels to prepare the way for Christ's second coming.

Hegai

Jesus said, "And there are eunuchs who have made themselves eunuchs for the kingdom of heaven's sake" (Matthew 19:12). One such eunuch was John the Baptist. He remained celibate in order to give himself wholeheartedly to the kingdom of God.

In ancient times, kings would surround themselves with many eunuchs. In fact, there were certain responsibilities with which eunuchs alone were entrusted. We see this clearly in the Book of Esther. King Ahasuerus of Persia had many eunuchs in his service, but the foremost eunuch was a man by the name of Hegai.

Hegai is introduced in the following verse: "Now when the turn came for Esther the daughter of Abihail the uncle of Mordecai, who had taken her as his daughter, to go in to the king, she requested nothing but what Hegai the king's eunuch, the custodian of the women, advised. And Esther obtained favor in the sight of all who saw her" (Esther 2:15).

Here's the background to this verse. King Ahasuerus had launched a search for a new Queen, and many young virgins from across the land had been brought into the palace and were being prepared to meet the King. The woman of his choosing would become Queen. Esther was one of the selected virgins, and she was undergoing many months of beauty treatments in preparation for her presentation to King Ahasuerus. Hegai, the king's eunuch, was in charge of this preparatory process.

King Ahasuerus placed a eunuch as custodian over Esther for one very specific reason: he was safe company for the Queen. As a eunuch, Hegai would have no personal desires toward Esther whom he served. He could serve her in the most intimate fashion without ever desiring her for himself.

Spiritual Eunuchs

God is raising up "spiritual eunuchs" in this hour. I do not mean He is simply raising up those who will take a vow of sexual abstinence. More than that, **He is raising up "spiritual eunuchs" who will have had cut away from their lives every desire for the attention and affections of people**. He will be able to entrust to these "spiritual eunuchs" the most sacred and intimate task of preparing the Bride for her wedding day.

Because of the cutting away that has taken place in their hearts, these leaders will be qualified to prepare the Bride for Christ's return. They will have no desire for the affections of the Bride.

But in order to serve the King in this most intimate way, these leaders will have known the excruciating pain of having everything cut away from them that remotely desires the praise of man. Instead of desiring human affirmation and recognition, these leaders will only desire to do the pleasure of their Lord.

These spiritual eunuchs will be true friends of the Bridegroom.

18

FRIENDSHIP WITH GOD: THE PAIN AND THE GLORY

"But what did you go out to see? A prophet? Yes, I say to you, and more than a prophet. For this is he of whom it is written: 'Behold, I send My messenger before Your face, who will prepare Your way before You.' Assuredly, I say to you, among those born of women there has not risen one greater than John the Baptist; but he who is least in the kingdom of heaven is greater than he" (Matthew 11:9-11).

Jesus said that John was "more than a prophet." It seems to me that he displayed all of the five-fold giftings. He functioned as an apostle, a prophet, an evangelist, a teacher, and even pastor (see Ephesians 4:11). He was mightily gifted and anointed. And yet Jesus said, "he who is least in the kingdom of heaven is greater than he."

I'm a long way from fully understanding that statement of Christ, but I see this much: There are those who aren't highly gifted or anointed by God. They are very simple people, they may not have many leadership skills, and perhaps the best they can do is serve in a corner — maybe mopping the floor, or cleaning the toilets. But even though these servants are not highly talented, they

do what they can do, faithfully loving the Lord in purity and sim-
plicity, using the very little they have to wash the feet of Jesus. In
heaven, that kind of love will be considered great and will be rewarded greatly because it wasn't a love that was kindled by a desire to attain great accomplishments.

They didn't love Jesus because He gave them a ministry, or a
following, or honor among men. They just loved Jesus because of
who He is. They could have wished for more, but they served God
faithfully without self-pity or bitterness, even though the best they
could do was the most menial of tasks. Their faithfulness had nothing to do with ministry function but had only to do with relationship. They didn't serve because of human recognition but because
their hearts were His. In eternity, the Lord will affirm that kind of
love as the greatest.

I am discovering it's possible to be successful before men but
barren before God. The Lord is teaching me that my sense of suc-
cess is to be found in His presence. When I am relating to Him in
abandoned love I am successful. Period. Ministry accomplishments can deceive me into thinking they are the measure of God's
approval on my life. There is a place in God where I really can gain
my sense of identity and fulfillment by worshiping Him and gazing
upon His face. I've caught a glimpse of this, and I'm after it with
all my heart.

The Place Of Greatness

What made John the Baptist the greatest prophet of all time? It
was nothing in John that made him the greatest prophet, because
we can look in the Bible and find other prophets who had much
more spectacular ministries. Elijah and Elisha saw incredible
miracles and supernatural signs through their ministries, and John
had no miracles. Isaiah and Jeremiah wrote books of the Bible;
John wrote none. Moses had overpowering encounters with the
visible, awesome glory of God — John never experienced anything
that dramatic in his lifetime.

So what made John the Baptist the greatest prophet of all time?
It was this: He was the forerunner of the Lord Jesus. Because he
served the feet of Jesus, he was the greatest prophet. **Greatness is**

found in proximity to Jesus. This is what made the twelve "apostles of the Lamb" so great and distinct from all other apostles: they served the Bridegroom. So their greatness had nothing to do with who they were but with who Jesus is. He is the Great One! He is the altogether glorious Bridegroom!

In the kingdom, it's not what you know but Who you know. God gives preferential treatment to His sons. It's like the business owner who might have several employees more qualified for the position, but who does he pick to succeed him as General Manager? His own son. Jesus didn't have to do anything to get the Father to be with Him. He didn't have to pass any tests; He didn't have to accomplish anything; the Father was with Him from day one because of their relationship.

The disciples were able to move out in healing and deliverance ministry, not because of what they had learned or attained but because of their proximity of relationship to Jesus. It's interesting to note that the one time they can't minister effectively to a demoniac, it's at a time when Jesus has gone away and is on the Mount of Transfiguration with Peter, James, and John. The other disciples begin to feel the absence of Jesus, even as the Israelites felt the absence of Moses when he stayed up on Mt. Sinai for forty days to be with God. In Moses' absence, the Israelites ended up erecting a golden calf. The disciples didn't fashion a gold calf while Jesus was on the mountain, but they did lose it. They felt distant from Jesus and thus were unable to cast the demon out of the boy.

The Lord will only work with those who remain close to Him. The Old Testament prophets were simply men who knew God. They were devoted to the presence and face of God. Elijah had this expression when referring to the Lord: "before whom I stand." Above all else, Elijah was a man who lived in the presence of God. An important ingredient to doing kingdom exploits is to stay close to the feet of Jesus. Those who really know Him do get preferential treatment.

Preferential Treatment

So you want to be God's friend, do you? Do you want to be a John the Baptist, wear camel's hair, and eat locusts and wild honey?

Do you want to be imprisoned in the prime of your life, and then cut off from the land of the living? You may want to reconsider, and look at how God treats His friends.

It's quite illuminating to study the lives of the prophets and see how God treats His friends. For starters, look at Jeremiah. Jeremiah lived a very unhappy life, in worldly terms that is. He paid a high price in loneliness because of his willingness to accept the divine call. He was reproached, ostracized, persecuted, misunderstood, "a man of strife and a man of contention to the whole earth" (Jeremiah 15:10). (It's interesting to note that many of the Jews thought Jesus was Jeremiah come back again, which shows they acknowledged the reproach and ostracization that Christ experienced.)

Jeremiah was not permitted to take a wife or to have children (Jeremiah 16:2); he wasn't allowed to attend funerals (16:5); he wasn't allowed to go to parties (16:8); he couldn't even attend weddings (16:9). His social life was lousy! There was only one source of joy in Jeremiah's life: "Your words were found, and I ate them, and Your word was to me the joy and rejoicing of my heart; for I am called by Your name, O LORD God of hosts" (Jeremiah 15:16). On the human level Jeremiah appeared to live a very underprivileged lifestyle, but at the internal level he knew the incredible joy of feasting on God's words. There is a joy in eating the words of God's mouth that exceeds that of all other earthly joys combined. Jeremiah had tapped into a dimension of love relationship with God that was worth all the pain that the rejection and resistance brought him.

God's Kind Of Love

There's another prophet in the Bible who was totally surrendered and consecrated to the purposes of God, and he paid a steep price as a result. Because of his abandonment to God, God came to him and said, "I'm going to kill your wife." Before you read any further, can you guess whose wife the Lord killed because of this man's consecration and obedience to God?

He was a great prophet and a true friend of God. But he paid a very high personal price to be used of the Lord. I'm referring to the prophet Ezekiel. You can read the story in Ezekiel 24, of how God snuffed out his wife's life. Not only did God kill Ezekiel's wife, but then God proceeded to tell Ezekiel how he was to handle his grief. God told him:

> "Son of man, behold, I take away from you the desire of your eyes with one stroke; yet you shall neither mourn nor weep, nor shall your tears run down. Sigh in silence, make no mourning for the dead; bind your turban on your head, and put your sandals on your feet; do not cover your lips, and do not eat man's bread of sorrow." So I spoke to the people in the morning, and at evening my wife died; and the next morning I did as I was commanded (Ezekiel 24:16-18).

What incredible consecration when a man is so surrendered to God that God can even take his wife away from him, and he continues to serve God with devotion and passion! Some of the people who suffered the most in the Bible had the greatest anointing on their lives. Their willingness to embrace the anointing of death qualified them to share in Christ's sufferings as they travailed together with all creation for the release of God's glory in the earth.

So you want to be God's friend. Are you sure? He doesn't treat His friends like men treat their friends. Paul realized this, because when he said he wanted to know Him, he realized he'd have to get to know Him in the fellowship of sharing in His sufferings, being conformed to His death. Because there's really no other way to get to know Him. If you want to be Jesus' friend, you must go with Him to the cross. If a great revelation of Christ has come to you, know this: great pain is also about to come to you. **You cannot see God without paying a great price personally**. Ezekiel discovered this. O what glory he saw, caught up into the very heavens! But God killed his wife, and gave him very painful relationships with his Jewish elders. Jesus knew God best and suffered the most. Look at the prophets, and for all their knowing of God and insight into His glory, they were among the most persecuted, harassed, misunderstood, rejected, lonely people on the face of the planet. God called Abraham His friend because he was willing to kill his only son. Hosea had to marry a harlot who would spurn Hosea's love and faithfulness and desert him. Paul had an incredible revelation of Christ, but he also had the suffering to match (2 Corinthians 11:24-28). **Friendship with God is a pathway of pain, but also of great glory.**

The Glory Of God

Why did these men endure such pain? Because they had tapped into an inner wellspring, they had an inner life with God in which the glory of God maintained, refreshed, and energized them.

O the joy of knowing the glory of God! O the delight of intimacy with His face. Even the roughest personalities disintegrate in the presence of God's manifest glory.

Simon Peter is a great example here. It's fascinating to notice what happened to Peter on the Mount of Transfiguration. Moses and Elijah appeared with Jesus in glory, and Peter saw it all. When Moses and Elijah began to depart, Peter just had to speak up. Let's read the account again:

> But Peter and those with him were heavy with sleep; and when they were fully awake, they saw His glory and the two men who stood with Him. Then it happened, as they were parting from Him, that Peter said to Jesus, "Master, it is good for us to be here; and let us make three tabernacles: one for You, one for Moses, and one for Elijah"— not knowing what he said (Luke 9:32-33).

Peter was so enraptured with the glory of God that he tried to prolong the glory by suggesting that Jesus postpone the closing of the meeting. He was so caught up (inebriated) in the glory of God that he didn't even know what he was saying.

Now, Peter was not one of these effusive, emotive, gushy-weepy types. He was a rather coarse, rough, opinionated, confrontative, impulsive, outspoken fellow, with a prophetic sort of personality. In other words, he wasn't the kind of guy that wanted unending prayer meetings (he kept falling asleep at the most important one), long worship services, just loving to hang out in the presence of God. But here's matter-of-fact, let's-get-on-with-it Peter, so caught up in the glory of God that he just wants to build some tents right there so they can all keep the meeting going.

Peter is so overcome with the touch of God's glory that he's reduced to a blubbering mess. Even as the glory of God melted tough-as-nails Peter in this way, the Lord wants to melt your heart as well with the glory of His manifest presence. It is this well-spring of glory that He opens up to His most intimate friends. There is no price tag too high for living in the glorious presence of our Lord Jesus. Bring on the pain, it is a light and momentary afflic-tion. We are His friends, and we are destined for great glory!

Section Five

THE
SONG
OF
SOLOMON

19

BEGINNING FERVENCY

"Ask Of Me"

At some point in the eternal councils of the Godhead, when the plan of redemption was being formulated in the wisdom of God, the Father determined an inheritance for His Son. This is reflected in Psalm 2:8, where the Father is speaking to His only begotten Son, and He says, "Ask of Me, and I will give You the nations for Your inheritance, and the ends of the earth for Your possession." The Father is telling His Son that He will give Him an inheritance in the nations, a people called out from the nations of the world who will be totally His. In fact, the Father is saying, "These people will be so completely Yours that You will have the affections of their heart, their soul, their mind, and their strength. You will possess the entirety of their being."

The Father is speaking of the church, and He is describing the depth and intensity of passion that the church will have for the Son of God. It's the love and devotion of the Bride for the heavenly Bridegroom.

The Son Asks

During Jesus' ministry on earth, the point came when Jesus actually called upon the promise of Psalm 2. We see this at the end of His ministry, just before He embraces the Father's cup. He is with His disciples, offering up what we call His "High Priestly prayer" in John 17 — the last words of Jesus that Scripture records before Gethsemane — and He ends that prayer with a very important statement. These are the last words of a Man who knows He's about to die. He's not wasting words, but He's expressing the depths of the passions of His heart because these are His last moments with His disciples.

Look with me at the last verse in Jesus' final prayer: "And I have declared to them Your name, and will declare it, that the love with which You loved Me may be in them, and I in them" (John 17:26). Here's what Jesus, in essence, is saying, "Father, You promised Me an inheritance among the nations, if I'd ask. You told Me You were going to prepare a Bride that would love Me with the kind of love with which You love Me. You said I only had to ask, and you'd give Me a people who would be so committed to Me that they would love Me with the very love of God. So I'm asking, Father. Give Me this Bride!"

Jesus' last great cry before His passion was for His promised Bride. "I'm praying that she not forget Me, Father, and that she not be distracted by the pursuit of this world, but that she love Me like You love Me Father!"

In this verse, Jesus also reveals how this love will be awakened in the hearts of His people, and it's through the revelation of the Father. Jesus is saying, "Father, I have declared Your name to them; I've shown them Your character and nature, and after I've ascended to Your throne I will continue to reveal Your name to them through the ministry of the Holy Spirit. And as they see You, I know that they will be quickened with a holy love for Me." When we touch the love of the Father through the Spirit of revelation, our hearts are awakened to true bridal affections for the Lord Jesus.

To Be His Inheritance

It's a marvelous thing when Jesus becomes our possession, but there's something even more glorious that Jesus is looking for, and that's when we become His possession. The apostle Paul points to this in Ephesians 1, when he writes, "**In Him also we have obtained an inheritance**, being predestined according to the purpose

of Him who works all things according to the counsel of His will"
(Eph. 1:11). It's true that we have a fantastic inheritance in Christ,
and multiplied thousands of sermons have been dedicated to this
glorious truth. But Paul doesn't stop there. He continues a few
verses later, "the eyes of your understanding being enlightened;
that you may know what is the hope of His calling, what are the
riches of the glory of **His inheritance in the saints**" (Eph. 1:18).
Paul takes some time to talk about their inheritance in Christ, but
then he prays that they'll move past that and grow into the even
greater understanding of what it means to be Christ's inheritance.

Jesus is looking for something in you. He wants to give out to
you, bless you, heal you, restore you, etc., but it's all for the purpose of eventually bringing you to the place where you live to touch
His heart. It's beyond our ability to comprehend, but there is something that God doesn't have. You have something that God the Son
doesn't have and that He greatly desires. It's the fully voluntary
love of the Bride for her Beloved. The extravagantly lavish passion of the church for the Lord Jesus is His rightful inheritance.

Beginning Fervency

The theme of John 17:26 is expanded for us in an entire book
of the Bible — the Song of Solomon. The Song of Solomon lays
out in eight chapters how the Lord fulfills John 17:26 in our hearts.
Mike Bickle describes this book as "The Progression of Holy Passion." It lays out the pattern of God's dealings in fervent believers
as He takes them step by step from self-centered Christianity to
God-centered Christianity. This section is dedicated to outlining
very briefly the major themes of this fascinating book, to help us
see with broad strokes how the Lord leads us into full and mature
bridal love. I suggest you read the chapters of this section with
your Bible open to the Song Of Solomon.

The Song of Solomon shows how the Lord matures the fervency of His people. He does it by revealing three things about
Himself: 1) He reveals the beauty of His person; 2) He affirms our
progress with His lavish affections; and 3) He lets us experience
the delightful sweetness of intimacy with Him. These three things
continually draw the Bride forward into increasingly abandoned
love and obedience. This is true mature love — when all other
affections have been completely abandoned for the love of the Son
of God and the delight of doing His will.

The book begins with the great bridal cry, "Let him kiss me with the kisses of his mouth" (1:2). This is the deep cry that the Holy Spirit is birthing in the Church in this hour, "Oh Lord Jesus, give me the intimacy of the kisses of Your mouth!" Then the Shulamite expresses her two-fold life vision: "Draw me away! We will run after you" (1:4). She is saying that she lives only for two things: for the ecstacy of being drawn away with Him in intimacy, and for the delight of running with Him in active ministry in the nations. **She wants to find the proper balance between intimacy and service,** but it's going to take several chapters for her to find it. He has placed this prayer deep in her heart, and the rest of the book is the unfolding development of how He draws her into intimacy in the midst of active servanthood. This is her life's goal, but it is not yet her attainment.

This two-fold goal of her life is summarized in the great commandment: to love God ("draw me away"), and to serve one's neighbor ("we will run after you"). At times there can be a very real tension between these two interests, characterized most famously in the personalities of Mary and Martha. Mary just wanted to love; Martha just wanted to serve, and as a result they clashed. **The zeal to serve can sometimes distract us from the intimacy of relationship Jesus longs to have with us.**

At the beginning of the book, the maiden is fervent but immature. This is an important distinction because fervency is not maturity. However, if you're not fervent, you'll never mature. Fervency opens up the pathway to maturity. **Fervency is the means; maturity is the goal.** Fervency must remain with us through every step of our Christian journey if we are to mature into complete bridal love.

20

HER SPIRITUAL JOURNEY BEGINS

Mistreatment From Christians

Early in her Christian walk the Bride experiences the jealousy of others in the body of Christ who are not as fervent as she is. They're angry at her (1:6) because her zeal for Jesus is making them look bad. So they put her to work in the vineyards, hoping to squelch her youthful fervency. Because of her desire to please the Lord, she ends up overextending and not properly nurturing her own relationship with Christ.

In her frustration, she overreacts a little bit and says, "Forget it, I'm not going to run anymore. All I want, Jesus, is to be with You" (see 1:7).

He responds by coming to her and comforting her. He says, "It's okay; everything's going to be all right because I love you. As far as I'm concerned, you're absolutely beautiful" (see 1:8-10). So He heals her with His affirmations of affection. The revelation of how much He loves us is **the** healing balm when we've known the pain of rejection.

Spiritual Pleasure

Because of the harsh way she was treated in the body of Christ, the Lord allows her to come aside and just be with Him for a while. He wants to completely win her heart by showing her the delight of His countenance. **He's treating her as He does many young be-**

lievers: He opens up to her the glory of His presence and allows her to experience the delight of His love. She is in the "honeymoon season" with Christ.

The first couple chapters describe it this way: She's behind a protective wall, on a bed, under an apple tree, at a table, and she's eating cakes with raisins. The Lord is embracing her on the bed, and she is totally intoxicated with His love. She is saying things like, "Jesus, You are so sweet! I just love-love-love You!" She has discovered why she was created. "I've found the purpose for living!" she cries. She is experiencing the glory of the Lord, and I mean, He is laying it on thick.

Here in the early days of her fervency, she is actually tasting of the depths of spiritual pleasure that God has designed for every believer. She is realizing that there is no pleasure equal to the pleasure of being moved upon by the Holy Spirit. She doesn't know it, but He's getting her hooked for life. She's getting addicted to God's glory and to the sweet wine of fellowshipping with the Holy Spirit.

In several places throughout the book, the Lord Jesus comes to her and reveals a new aspect of His personhood. The first revelation she has of Him is right here: she sees Him as the affectionate, loving, soul-satisfying, sweet Savior. He is much more than that, but this is all she knows right now. As far as she is concerned, **this** is Christianity. She feels so very blessed, and she's convinced this is how it should always be. She is self-absorbed, however, and doesn't know it. Her chief goal in life right now is to be blessed, to enjoy the Lord, and to feel His presence. She does not yet have a passion to do His will. She is fervent but immature.

In 2:7, the Lord as much as says to those who know her, "Yes, I know she's self-absorbed right now and that's she's cut herself off from the body for a season, but leave her alone. I'm doing something very important in her. If she is to grow into full maturity, she has got to experience the pleasure of intimate communion with Me. Don't bother her right now."

First Stage Of Maturity

The progression of her maturity is seen in four "phases" or "stages" in the Song Of Solomon. Her first stage of maturity is depicted in 1:13-14 — "A bundle of myrrh is my beloved to me, that lies all night between my breasts. My beloved is to me a cluster of henna blooms in the vineyards of En Gedi." Twice in these phrases she says, "My Beloved is **to me**." In other words, she's saying, "He's mine, all mine!" As far as she's concerned, God exists for her. Her immaturity is seen in her self-absorption. And yet the Lord loves her fervency and enjoys her in her immaturity.

Right now she sees Him only as her inheritance, but He wants her to become His inheritance. **Her goal is to feel God's presence, but His goal is to make her a co-equal partner that will run with Him in intimacy and servanthood to do warfare in the nations.** She's feeling like, "As long as You embrace me with one hand, and pop raisin cakes in my mouth with Your other hand, I will love You totally, and tell everybody about You." His question of her, however, is, "What will you do when I turn it around and I extract from you the fact that you are My inheritance — that I don't just exist for you, but that you exist for Me?" She isn't even close to being ready to face that issue at this point.

You see, the ultimate goal of Christianity is not, in the final analysis, to enjoy God — even though the enjoyment of God is essential. **The goal of Christianity is to be the inheritance of Christ Jesus and to love him with full obedience.**

Her Disobedience

In 2:8f, Jesus comes to her and challenges her to leave her comfort zone. He shows Himself to her like a gazelle who leaps on mountains and skips on hills, and this is an entirely new side of Him that she's never seen before. She's only known Him as her lover on the bed, and she's not comfortable with this new face He's revealing of Himself. This is her second revelation of Him — she is seeing Him as the King of the Nations.

Generally, mountains in the Bible typify three things: obstacles, demonic powers, and nations. She is seeing Jesus as King of the nations who leaps over every obstacle and challenge with absolute ease, and He invites her to join Him in His triumphal procession. He's saying, "Come with Me; let's conquer the nations together."

She says, "Why are you doing all this leaping stuff? Come back to bed! The music is perfect, the food is great, and it's just

You and me. Come here and pop another raisin cake into my mouth."

He says, "You've been on the bed long enough. Rise up and come with Me. Let's take on the mountains together. Learn to run with Me in the nations."

In the end, she's actually going to tell the Lord "no." In 2:17 she's basically going to say, "I don't like mountain climbing. Come back to bed; we had a good thing going." Since He's intent on leaping on mountains, she ends up telling Him to turn and go by Himself. For her part, she's staying behind the protective wall, under the shade tree, on the bed.

Her disobedience is rooted not so much in rebellion as it is in fear. She's afraid to get off the bed she knows in order to run with Him over mountains she's never scaled before. She still longs for Him desperately but she's afraid to leave her safe surroundings. She has yet to learn that it's safer to be walking out on the stormy water with Jesus than to be in the boat without Him.

But even though she's in disobedience at this point in her walk, she's beginning to recognize something, and she gives expression to it in 2:16, "My Beloved is mine and I am His." This statement reflects "phase 2" of her progression in holy passion. In "phase 1" she was saying, "He's mine, He's mine." Now she is saying, "He's my inheritance, no question, but I am seeing for the first time that He's claiming an inheritance in me." She's not ready to be that inheritance for Him, but she's catching a vision for the kind of commitment that He's wanting to extract from her.

His Chastisement

Since she has said "no" to Him in 2:17, she's going to come under divine chastisement in Chapter Three. He loves her too much to let her stay in disobedience. He's going to pry her fingers loose from the things that keep her in bondage. In 2:17 she basically said, "Turn, go by Yourself; I'm staying in bed." So in Chapter Three He does just that: He turns and removes from her the awareness of His presence. (He never actually leaves her, but He does withdraw her ability to sense His presence.)

She is totally unprepared for Him to withdraw His presence, and she cries out her distress in 3:1, "AHH! I can't live like this! I was created to know Your presence. God, where are You?" She's willing to do anything to ease the pain, so in 3:2 she says, "Okay, I'll get out of bed." She has touched too much of God to live without His smile. She agrees to get off her bed of self-absorption, and she goes out to the city. The city is where people are, so she is accepting the Lord's call to reach out to others. She's hooked. She'll do anything to find the sweetness of His presence again. So she's beginning to embrace the second commandment — to love others as herself.

Her obedience is quickly rewarded in 3:4, and He renews the sense of His presence. She learns that she will know His presence only as she reaches beyond herself to others. She feels like she's really starting to master this thing called obedience, but she doesn't realize how much she still has to learn. She doesn't realize there are many areas of her heart that are not fully surrendered to the Lord. And He isn't going to be satisfied until He possesses her fully — in thought, word, and deed. He's looking for more than external acts of obedience; He's wanting to conquer every chamber of her inner being.

The Shelter Of His Presence

As she returns to serving others in the church, she's afraid because the last time she served in the church she got hurt. So now in 3:6-11, Jesus gives her an awesome revelation of the absolute security of serving Him. "Where I am," He says in 3:7, "there is absolute safety." She realizes He will protect her as she returns to where the people are.

She wants to object, "But they treated me so badly, I don't want to be with them." But He assures her, "You need to understand, it's My body; it's the only one I have on the earth. If you want to be with Me, that's where I am."

She comes to the realization that even though being in the body of Christ may be painful at times, ultimately it's the only safe place to be. And He begins to show her His glorious perspective on the church. Her commitment to the church is the thing that opens to her the glorious dimensions that await her.

21

SHE EMBRACES HIS DISCIPLINES

Equipped for Spiritual Warfare

In 4:1-5, He begins to equip her for spiritual warfare, and the way He does it is really incredible. He does it by telling her how He views her. He's going to begin to pour His affection upon her and call her forth by affirming the wonderful things He sees in her, even though they are only beginning to appear in her life. He begins to call forth her virtues as though they were fully formed.

Yes, He disciplines her — but He wraps it in profuse affirmation. He motivates her with love rather than with judgment. She is blown away by how Jesus views her in her sincerity and fervency, even though she is weak and struggling. He sees how she longs for Him in the midst of her frailty and fears, and His heart melts!

This is one of the chief ways Jesus awakens passion and love in the hearts of His people: He expresses His passion for them. You will never be more passionate for Him than the revelation you carry of His passion for you. **When you see how much God enjoys you, something is set free in your heart to enjoy Him like you never have before**.

Amazingly, He speaks over her life as though she were fully mature. He sees glorious qualities in her that are only in seed form, and He extols them as though they were full-grown. He speaks prophetically over her life according to what He sees her becoming, and this is how He calls her forward into greater maturity. He declares her readiness to do battle long before she herself feels ready.

Her Increasing Consecration

His profuse affection totally melts her heart. In 4:6 she responds to Him, "If my obedience wins this kind of affection from you, then okay, I **will** embrace the call of 2:10. I **will** go to the mountain!" And here she recognizes it as "the mountain of myrrh." Myrrh is a burial spice, and it was used in Jesus' burial. Thus, myrrh in the Bible can be seen as a symbol of the cross. In 4:6 she is saying yes to the mountain of myrrh — Mount Calvary — the cross. She is saying, "I'll go all the way. I'll embrace Your death."

This is an awesome moment in her pilgrimage. When she says "yes" to the cross, the whole book shifts gears. Everything changes. Her willingness to embrace the cross produces a most powerful response from Him. When she says she's willing to be obedient even unto death, something flips inside His heart, and He comes back with an incredible deluge of affection. This is her turning point in the book.

In verses 7-15, He proceeds to dizzy her with a veritable litany of affection and delight. It's here that we come to the main verse of the entire book: "You have ravished my heart, my sister, my spouse; you have ravished my heart with one look of your eyes, with one link of your necklace" (4:9). For the first time He calls her "My spouse," and He says, "You have ravished My heart." She's not perfect by any means, and she has only expressed a willingness to embrace the cross, but He is ravished over her. If there's anything we need a greater understanding of, it's how Jesus views us when we're making sincere commitments to serve Him, even though we sometimes fail. He sees our shortcomings, but because of the fervency of our hearts and sincere desire to walk in obedience, He is ravished by just one look of our eyes!

And make no mistake, His love is sweeping her off her feet! He dizzies her with His torrent of affirmation. She is so captured by His affections for her that she makes an absolutely incredible statement. **She is coming to the conclusion that if He loves her this much, then it's safe to obey Him.** She decides that anything that comes from His hand is for her good because she realizes how ravished He is over her. She has seen His love for her, and she is about to commit herself to absolute, unequivocal obedience — because she realizes that her obedience is the only thing that opens her heart to discovering more of His beauty.

Before we look at her incredible statement to which I've referred, let me remind you of the two levels of obedience she has already embraced. The first stage of obedience was in 3:2 when she rose up and began to reach out to other people in their needs. The second stage of obedience was in 4:6 when she embraced the mountain of myrrh (the cross). And now she commits to a third level of obedience in 4:16 as she says, "Awake, O north wind." Here's the incredible thing she's saying: "That's it! If embracing the cross gets this kind of affection from You, then I'm 100% Yours. Whatever it takes. Do whatever it takes for my heart to be totally Yours." Now **that's** dangerous praying!

Inviting The Ultimate Test

In 4:16 she invokes the north winds and south winds. The north winds are the bitter cold winds of winter. It's almost unbelievable, but she's actually praying, "Let the winter season come!" She is inviting a level of God's dealings in her life that He isn't even requiring of her. But she's not a masochist, so she also asks for some south winds of blessing and refreshing to come from time to time or else she wouldn't survive. Most saints pray or rebuke the north winds away, but she is so captured by His love that she is completely abandoning herself to His purposes.

To illustrate how God uses winter seasons in our lives, let me use the example of our New York State highways. Before winter hits, our N.Y. roads appear to be in excellent condition, ready for the rigors of winter. But there are small fissures, cracks, and imperfections in the pavement which are not visible to the naked eye. Water finds its way into the hidden cracks and flaws, and then freezes in the cold. When the water freezes, it expands, pushing the pavement apart. Soon, large potholes appear everywhere. The weaknesses were there all along, but it wasn't until the cold of winter that the fault lines beneath the surface became evident. In a similar way, God takes us through winter seasons (spiritually) to reveal the hidden imperfections of our hearts that we couldn't see before. You can't deal with something until you see it.

The north wind represents the winds of adversity and crisis, and the south wind represents the refreshing winds of the Holy Spirit. All of us prefer the warm summer winds of the Holy Spirit's quickening, but the cold winds of calamity are equally necessary at the proper times in our lives. It has been my observation in the current stirrings of the Holy Spirit that both the north and south winds are blowing across the land. Those in the summer season are being refreshed with laughter and drunkenness in the Spirit; those in the winter season are being devastated with calamity and crisis. Both winds are of God and are equally necessary for the harvest He is cultivating in our lives. If you're in the cold of winter, don't become envious over those who are enjoying the warm summer breezes of the Holy Spirit. As surely as that person will someday feel the north wind, so too you will soon enjoy the south wind.

So at this point in her walk the Bride is saying, "Awake oh north winds. I know that I am so safe in Your love, Lord, that I'll be able to handle anything You might have to do to reveal the hidden flaws in my life that keep me from being Your full possession. If You touch an area of my life, I know it's because You will make me to become the full inheritance that Your Father promised You." In 4:16b she acknowledges that her life is His garden, and she knows that the winter season is necessary if the spices that He enjoys are to flow from her life.

He sees the sincerity of her cry to be totally His, and so even though she doesn't fully realize what she has asked for, He decides to answer her prayer and send the north winds. That's what happens in Chapter Five. He takes her through the greatest test of her life. In Chapter Three she was disciplined because of her disobedience, but now she's going to be disciplined because of her obedience.

The Two-Fold Test Of Maturity

We now come to Chapter Five where she enters the greatest test of her life. Jesus reveals Himself to her in 5:2 in an entirely new way. Coming to her with dew-covered hair, He is the Jesus of the Garden of Gethsemane. He is going to lead her into what the Mystics have called "the dark night of the soul."

This ultimate test has two prongs to it. It begins with a "spiritual blackout" — she loses all awareness of God's presence in her life (5:6). She finds herself in a place of spiritual trauma, and every effort to find God is met with futility. Heaven is shut up, totally silent. No amount of faith or repentance or obedience changes anything. She feels like God has forsaken her, and she has absolutely no idea why.

But there's still more pain to come. The second half of the test involves her relationships in the body of Christ. In 5:7 the watchmen strike her, wound her, and remove her veil. The watchmen are leaders in the body of Christ, and they wound her with their words because they don't understand what's happening to her. They sincerely want to help her, but they don't have the discernment to realize what God is doing in her. They say to her things like, "There must be sin in your life. You need to repent." They not only hurt her with their undiscerning words, but they even remove her veil — her spiritual covering. This often represents a temporary or partial removal from ministry.

At this point, everything she lives for has been taken from her. All she ever wanted was two things: to be drawn into His presence in intimacy, and to run with Him in ministry service (1:4). Now, both of these things are stripped from her. She has no sense of His presence, and she is not free to function in ministry as she was before. Some readers will find themselves really relating to the Bride at this point because this is a commonly experienced part of God's divine pattern in cultivating holy passion within His fervent ones.

Here's what God is trying to accomplish in her: He removes the sense of His presence because He wants to determine, "Do you love Me because of the pleasure you gain in My presence? Are you in this thing for Me or for yourself? Will you still love Me even if you no longer enjoy Me?"

And secondly, He removes her from active ministry because He's wondering, "Do you love to serve Me because it meets some ego need in yourself and because it satisfies your need for feelings of significance? Will you be Mine even if I don't anoint you? Are you Mine even if I let leaders who you honor touch you and test you?"

22

HIS AFFIRMATION

Her Response

She's going to come back with a great response. In essence she's going to say, "In the early days I loved You because of what You did for me. But I've seen You, and now I love You because of who You are."

This is most amazing. God seems to have abandoned her, the body of Christ is reproaching her, she is wounded and feels naked and exposed, and everything inside is screaming, "Run and hide! Get out of here!" But this time she doesn't leave. She stays in the body of Christ. Contrary to every impulse, she just stands there, without reviling her accusers, and pleads in 5:8, "I can't find my Beloved. He has left me. If you find Him, please tell Him that I am lovesick for Him!" She comes out of this test awesomely — with a tenacious love for her Beloved. She is truly becoming a mature Bride.

The other members of the body of Christ are mystified by her. They're thinking, "What's with you? After all He's done to you, Honey, we wouldn't fault you one bit for being angry with Him. He's forsaken you and caused you to be wounded by leaders you respected. But instead of being angry at Him, you're more lovesick than ever!" So in 5:9 they begin to wonder, "What is your Beloved more than another beloved, that you so charge us?" They're asking, "What is so wonderful about your Beloved, that you would still love Him like this after all He's put you through? We think He's admirable, but you must see something in Him that we don't see. We don't understand this kind of love. What do you see in Him?"

The following seven verses (5:10-16) are her reply, and they are an awesome description of the glory and beauty of the Lord Jesus. Each phrase is full of symbolic meaning. This is one of the most extravagant eulogies of Jesus in the entire Scriptures. **She feels like the presence of God has been removed from her life, but the Bride has been so captured by His love that even under great duress she is absolutely preoccupied with His beauty**. Far from being angry or disenchanted, she is swift to extol His virtues.

The other members of the body are so taken with her description of her Beloved that they begin to ask in 6:1, "If He is who you say He is, then where is He, that we can seek Him with you?" Her love has become an effective witness. Now others are being drawn toward the same fervent, extravagant relationship with the Beloved that she has.

It's at this point in the narrative that the Bride has come to the third phase of her spiritual progression. In 6:3 she says, "I am my Beloved's and my Beloved is mine." The order is reversed. Before, she was saying that He was hers, and she was His. Now she is recognizing that she is first and foremost His inheritance, and then of course He is hers as well. Her priorities have been radically revolutionized through the extreme test of Chapter Five. Above all, she wants to be totally His. This represents a complete change in her heart motivations.

The Beloved's Response

When the Lord sees this incredible change in her heart aspirations, He comes back to her with the most awesome declaration of affirmation you could ever imagine. He vindicates her before those who thought she was compromising and imbalanced. He cries out, "O my love, you are as beautiful as Tirzah, lovely as Jerusalem, awesome as an army with banners! Turn your eyes away from me, for they have overcome me" (6:4-5a).

"Awesome as an army with banners" — armies in those days would carry banners back to their capital city after a great victory.

He is describing her as a victorious army. He is saying, "You've been victorious over the enemies within. You've conquered the foes within your own heart that have led you away from pure love."

And then He looks at her and says, "Turn your eyes away from me, for they have overcome Me" (6:5). She couldn't feel His presence or affirmation for such a long time, and during that silent period she constantly wondered, "What does He think of me? Is He mad at me? Have I displeased Him somehow? Has He cast me aside?" And now He breaks the long silence and says to her, "Let Me tell you what I was thinking when you couldn't feel my presence. My heart was being ravished over you! You didn't understand what was happening to you, but you just stood there and loved Me anyways. I can't tell you how moved I am over you. Your love is so pure. Oh, turn your eyes from Me, I am overcome with the devotion of your love for Me!"

This is the Captain of the Lord's hosts speaking here. This is the King of kings and the Lord of lords who will one day destroy His enemies with the sheer splendor of His presence. All of earth's forces cannot stop Him. All of hell's powers cannot defeat Him. Nothing in heaven or earth can conquer Him. He cannot be overcome by anyone or anything — except this: this Bride who adores Him through her pain. Only one thing can overcome and conquer the heart of God the Son, and that is the Bride of Christ who loves Him when everything is against her.

I can hear Jesus saying to His Father, "Father, You did it. You promised Me a Bride from the nations who would love Me like You love Me. You said she would share My passions and heartbeat, and would carry My values. You said she and I would have many things in common, and here You've given Me a Bride who shares My cross. She's compatible to Me, she's so much like Me, and I love her so much. O holy Father, this is the Bride You promised Me! She is mature and prepared to be My co-equal partner, running with Me in the nations to bring in the harvest. Thank you, Father!"

Motivated By Grace

The Lord has poured such effusive praise and love upon her that she erupts in a response (6:11-12) that surprises even her. His affections have so inflamed her heart that she finds herself reaching out to the needs of the church with zeal like she's never experienced before. The imagery of these verses refers to the body of Christ and to the relative growth of individual believers. Instead of being exasperated with young, immature believers, she finds herself greatly interested in their spiritual welfare and continued growth in the Lord. She is seeing the same potential in the immature believers that the Lord saw in her.

As swift as a chariot, her soul is caught up with zeal for the work of God. Never before has she been able to love others with such an unconditional love — with the very love of God. She finds herself able to love angry, envious, ungrateful people. She now cares deeply for those in the body of Christ who once mistreated her. Her heart has been enlarged to care for the entire church. She recognizes that God, by His grace, is channelling a quality of love through her life that was not inherent to her personality.

Two Responses

As zeal fills her heart for the church, she encounters two responses. In 6:13a, sincere believers who appreciate what God has done in her call to her and say, "Come to us! Come help us." They see an anointing on her life to impart grace by the Spirit, and they want to receive from her.

The second half of 6:13 describes the response of cynical or jealous people in the church who don't acknowledge what God has done in her. Instead of affirming her, they are critical of her. They are offended by her zeal, and they say, "Listen, we don't think you people should have anything to do with her. She's legalistic, narrowminded, imbalanced, and she's a bad example. Why are you looking at her anyway?"

This is "the dance of the two camps." It's the tension that has always existed between sincere believers and insincere believers. There will always be an insincere church — those who don't want to be challenged to holiness and purity, to greater consecration, and to a deeper intimacy with the Lord Jesus. Saul and David have danced all through church history. The fervency and consecration of the Bride will always cause division in the church because there will always be those who won't like the conviction her presence brings.

She Is Vindicated

In 7:1-5, the sincere church begins to answer the question posed by the sarcastic church: "What would you see in the Shulamite?" They praise the virtues that are ever growing in her by the grace of God. They recognize that King Jesus is held captive by the glory of her attainments.

In 7:6-9, the Lord Himself vindicates her. He is ravished with the delights that her love brings Him. As a palm tree, she has grown to great stature. Her breasts are likened to palm tree clusters, referring to her ability to nurture spiritual babes in the milk of the word. He is validating her ministry.

23

FULLY MATURE LOVE

Final Phase

The fourth phase of her progression in holy passion is seen in 7:10: "I am my beloved's and his desire is for me." She is saying, "I am His, and He wants me for His own. I am His, I am His." She doesn't even mention the fact that He is hers. She knows what Jesus will do for her, but that truth is swallowed up in her new-found realization that she exists only for Him. She has progressed from the self-centered focus of 1:13-14 to the God-centered focus of 7:10.

The transition is complete. She has truly died to self and is alive only to God. Her only concern is that she be His inheritance. At this point her love is fully mature, and her life is able to be devoted to 100-fold fruitfulness in the Master's vineyard.

Cry For Intimacy In Service

Now we see the Bride longing to move out in active ministry with the Lord (7:11-13). Back in Chapter Two, when He had called her to rise from her bed of intimacy and run with Him in the nations, she had declined. Now, she's not only willing to move out in servanthood, she is actually initiating it.

She makes it clear, however, that she wants to go out to the harvest field **with Him**. So four times she says, "Let us." She's willing to pour her life out for others as long as she's in His presence.

In verse 12 she says, "There I will give you my love." She is saying, "There — in the place of active ministry — I will give You my love. I want to give You my abandoned affections in the midst of running in ministry." She has learned what it means to put intimacy and ministry function together.

Complete Dependence

Chapter Eight contains a glorious description of this fully matured Bride. "Who is this coming up from the wilderness, leaning upon her beloved?" (8:5). The change in her is so radical that she is barely recognizable. She is arising from her wilderness season victoriously, and the most outstanding quality of her life is that she is leaning upon her Beloved. Perhaps we might have expected the fully mature believer to be a spiritual giant, a veritable pillar, standing head and shoulders above others. But no, she can hardly even stand up. She has been so broken by the wilderness that she depends upon her Beloved for virtually every step. **This is the scriptural image of full bridal maturity: complete dependence**. God is bringing those who are willing, in this hour, to a place of brokenness, helplessness, weakness, and absolute dependence upon Him.

Covenant Commitment

Now the Lord Jesus comes to her and says, "Set me as a seal upon your heart, as a seal upon your arm" (8:6a). The Lord wants to seal her heart by the power of the Holy Spirit.

A seal preserves. For example, when a jar of jam seals we call it "preserves." The seal protects the contents in the jar so that the original strength of flavor is preserved. In a similar sense the Lord is saying, "Invite Me to preserve your love. Let Me bottle up your love so that no deteriorating bacteria can get in to spoil your love. If you set Me as a seal on your heart, I will preserve your love to the end."

The seal on her arm represents her commitment to move in the power of the Holy Spirit rather than the arm of the flesh.

The Fire Of God's Love

Song of Solomon 8:6 is where God's love is called a fire: "For love is as strong as death, jealousy as cruel as the grave; its flames are flames of fire, a most vehement flame." Death is our strongest enemy — stronger than sin or the devil — and is the final enemy that will be destroyed. There is an intensity of love that is so powerful, so all-consuming, that it is likened unto death itself.

Nothing in this life escapes the specter of death. It is an all-consuming reality that conquers all earthly life forms. In the same way, the love of God is absolutely consuming. **Death didn't take Jesus' life from Him, love did. God's love demands our all.** Even as nothing on earth is exempt from death's claims, so too those who surrender to the love of God will find everything in their lives being consumed — until all that remains is love.

"Its flames are flames of fire, a most vehement flame." The last phrase literally means, "A flame of YAH." There is no fire like the very fire of God. There is a love being kindled in the hearts of God's people today that is inflamed and energized by God Himself.

There is coming to the church in the last days a mighty revelation of the love of God. It will be so consuming that God is going to completely capture the hearts of His people for His Son. Before it's all over, the church is going to have a complete preoccupation with the Son of God. Everything we are will be His.

Sometimes when we look at the weaknesses of the church we wonder, "God, how are You going to make this church into something that is glorious, without spot or wrinkle?" We have inner wounds, emotional handicaps, addictions, bondages to sin, and we can't imagine God perfecting a people like us.

The Lord's answer is, "The issue is not your weakness — the issue is **My fire!** When I release the fire of my love in the earth, everything in you will change. I will awaken in you a love beyond anything you've ever experienced. You will see My Son!"

Whenever God wants to change anything on this planet, He just sends some fire. Sometimes it appears as though God's kingdom is advancing painfully slowly at times, but nothing can hinder the acceleration of His purposes when He turns up the fire.

This fire of God penetrates **anything**. A flame that's hot enough will melt steel like butter. God says, "The fire of My love is hot enough to melt every resistance in your soul." God's love will purify the most addicted, broken person, for this fire is the very flame of God Himself. There is no obstacle in this Bride's heart, no area of demonic stronghold, no corner of hidden rebellion, no scar of emotional wounding, that is able to withstand this flame. Every area of resistance in her heart and soul will be consumed. **Nothing will survive the jealous furnace of God's fiery love — nothing, that is, except love**.

Unquenchable Fire

"Many waters cannot quench love, nor can the floods drown it" (8:7a). Waters in the Bible often symbolize problems and difficulties that seek to overwhelm and drown us. This verse is saying, "There is no opposition great enough to quench this love for Jesus that burns in the hearts of God's saints."

Many saints in the Bible knew overwhelming circumstances, and many saints today continue to experience the deep floods of adversity and crisis. But even after Satan levels his greatest attacks, God's people come through with a deeper, more fiery love than ever. Revelation 12 depicts Satan (the dragon) in his last days' rage, spewing a flood from his mouth in order to try to drown the church, but he is not successful. When he spews forth his deepest waters upon God's people, the grace of God lifts up a standard against that flood. When the enemy would seek to drown us, the Lord kindles a fire within us that cannot be extinguished. It is a fiery love for the Lord Jesus.

In an hour when the saints are facing their greatest testings, the Lord is reserving a revelation of Himself and His beauty. He is saying to us, "Don't be afraid of or intimidated by the dragon's floods, because when I reveal Myself to you, the power of the revelation of My love will be stronger than the rage of Satan." God has a fire that will lick up and consume the greatest floods of the dragon — it's the very fire of God Himself.

Mountains Of Spices

The last two verses represent the final cry of the Lord Jesus and then of the Bride. Verse 13 is the Beloved's last request, and verse 14 is her last request.

In verse 13 Jesus is recognizing that she has become a fully mature partner with Him, for she is giving herself with abandonment to the harvest in the garden of God. But in the midst of her running in service He says, "Don't forget that I want to hear your voice." Although there are many others in the body of Christ that now want to hear from her, He reminds her that He also longs for intimate communion with her. He is admonishing her that in the midst of all her labors she must not neglect the place of intimacy with Him. This is the prayer of Chapter One all over again — "Draw me, and let us run." He loves the way she's serving, but He reminds her to keep the nurturing of their relationship in constant focus.

In verse 14 her last words are, "Make haste, my beloved, and be like a gazelle or a young stag on the mountains of spices." She is recognizing His sovereignty over the nations, and she is interceding for the final manifestation of Christ's victory. "Make haste" is another way of saying, "Come quickly!" (1 Corinthians 16:22, "maranatha"). In Revelation 22:20 she says it this way, "Even so, come, Lord Jesus!" She is crying for Christ's second coming.

The corporate church has been called in the book a "garden of spices" (4:16; 5:1; 6:2), but now for the first time we encounter this phrase, "the mountains of spices." This depicts the eternal city which is an abundance of diverse spices. The fragrant spices from every believer's life which have been cultivated on earth, compounded together, will become a veritable mountain of delightful spices that will be presented to the Lord Jesus on the final day.

Have you ever wondered why the Bride of Christ is so broadly diverse, comprised of multiplied millions of people, each with a totally unique personality? One reason is because the heart of Jesus is so incredibly deep and multifaceted that it will take that many saints to touch the fullness and profound complexity of Christ's heart. The fragrance of your life is an aroma that moves the heart of Christ like no one else can touch Him. As every member of the Bride offers his or her spices of affections to the Lord Jesus, together we comprise a mountain of spices to please His heart.

So this tremendous book ends with the Bride praying, "Lord Jesus, come quickly! Come and take us from this world, and be the stag that triumphs over every evil of this age. Take us up to glory so that you might rejoice upon this mountain — the Lamb's wife

— with its abundance of spices."
   Even so, come, Lord Jesus!

   (Author's note: I have received permission from Mike
   Bickle to print this section because I am borrowing heavily
   from his teaching. I highly commend Mike's in-depth
   teachings on this subject. His complete teaching resources
   on The Song Of Solomon are available from Abounding
   Grace Bookstore, PO Box 229, Grandview, MO 64030-
   0229, or by calling 1-800-552-2449.)

Section Six

THE GREATEST IS LOVE

24

GOD'S JEALOUS LOVE

"Set me as a seal upon your heart, as a seal upon your arm; for love is as strong as death, jealousy as cruel as the grave; its flames are flames of fire, a most vehement flame" (Song of Solomon 8:6).

In the last chapter we dealt with this verse (Song of Solomon 8:6), but we talked only about the fire of love. We didn't deal with its companion — the flame of jealousy. Love has another face to it, and it's called jealousy. The subject of God's jealousy is fearfully compelling, and deserves special attention (hence this brief chapter).

Wherever there is true love, there is jealousy. Within the marriage covenant, for example, the exclusivity of love demands a commensurate jealousy. If I truly love my wife, I am jealous over her that she not share her love with any other man.

Applying the symbolism of marriage to our relationship with God, God's love for us is like the love of a man for his wife, and it burns like a fire. But with His love comes His jealousy. I would venture to suppose that all my readers yearn to receive and enjoy the everlasting love of God. What we sometimes forget, however, is that when we get God's love we also get His jealousy.

Healthy Jealousy

There is a paranoid kind of jealousy that consumes some spouses. Some husbands are so suspicious of their wives that they are constantly grilling them, questioning every move they make, and trying to restrict their social life. I am not talking about that kind of unhealthy jealousy. That's not really jealousy; that's suspicion and distrust. True love "believes all things" (1 Corinthians 13:7).

There is a wholesome kind of jealousy that demands that true love not be shared with a third party. True love says, "I love you dearly, Sweetheart, but if this marriage is going to work, you're going to have to save your body and your passions exclusively for me."

In this best sense of the word, God is intensely jealous. He passionately desires that we not share our love with any other gods, so much so that He even says, "My name is Jealous" (see Exodus 34:14). Even as a husband has the right to the exclusive affections of his wife, God has the right to the exclusive affections of His people.

God's Cruel Jealousy

Song of Solomon 8:6 is simultaneously showing us both sides of God's love. His love for us is as strong as death, but His jealousy over us is as cruel as the grave. We want His love, but few are prepared for the intensity of His jealousy. And yet, you can't have God's love without His jealousy. **His love is wonderful, but His jealousy is cruel.**

When you pray Song of Solomon 8:6, "Come, Holy Spirit, seal my heart — cause my love to be true," then know two things: 1) you're opening your heart to a love that is stronger than death, and 2) you're opening your heart to a jealousy that is as cruel as the grave. So the Lord asks, "Do you understand that with My love comes My jealousy?"

God has a holy, righteous jealousy for His people. He longs for the affections of all men, but He is jealous over the affections of His Bride. When His people err in their hearts and become infatuated with other passions and delights, the jealousy of God is aroused.

It is a fearful thing to enter into covenant love with the holy God of the universe, and then have wandering eyes for other attractions.

"Wrath is cruel and anger a torrent, but who is able to stand before jealousy?" (Proverbs 27:4). This verse indicates that it's one thing to suffer the wrath of God as a sinner; it's quite another thing altogether to suffer the jealousy of God as a flirting, wayward, lukewarm believer. Thus Paul warns compromising Christians with these words, "Or do we provoke the Lord to jealousy? Are we stronger than He?" (1 Corinthians 10:22). He is asking, "Are you feeling strong enough to stir up the frightful cruelty of the Lord's jealousy?"

The Consequences Of Jealousy

The cruelty of God's jealousy has actually brought some believers to an early grave. 1 Corinthians 11:30 points to this, saying that some have fallen sleep (died) because they did not properly discern the body and blood of Christ. 1 Corinthians 5:5 also points to this, indicating that it's preferable for someone to be killed by God's jealousy and at least have their spirit saved than that they perish in a Christless eternity.

The ultimate cruelty of God's jealousy is seen in Revelation 3:15-16: "'I know your works, that you are neither cold nor hot. I could wish you were cold or hot. So then, because you are lukewarm, and neither cold nor hot, I will vomit you out of My mouth.'" I used to look at that verse, and in my natural understanding I would think, "Surely not, Lord! Surely you wouldn't look at someone who believed in you, and on that final day spew them from Your presence!" But I hadn't taken into account the fiery indignation of His jealousy.

Why would Jesus deal so forcefully with someone who believed Him but had just grown half-hearted in his love and commitment? The answer is seen in the cross of Christ. When you look at the cross, you see the blazing inferno of His fiery love. The cross cries out, "This is how hot My love is for you!" And from His cross He cries, "I want a Bride who loves Me with the same fervency and passion. I want a Bride who will love Me like I love her."

As you behold the cross and see His blazing love for you, do you think He'll be satisfied with a half-hearted, yawn-in-your-face kind of love in return? No! He'll vomit that kind of sickening love out of His mouth. **His love requires — demands — a burning purity of love in return that blazes with zeal for nothing but the face of Jesus Christ.**

Love Grown Cold

Jesus warned us that in the last days the love of many believers will become lukewarm: "And because lawlessness will abound, the love of many will grow cold" (Matthew 24:12). This is one of the great sicknesses of the church today. The more that lawlessness abounds, the more our love for Jesus tends to grow cold — for we are seduced and courted by the abounding lawlessness. Lawlessness says, "It's your thing, do what you want to do"; "To each his own"; "Do what's right for you." Lawlessness erases all absolutes and empowers the individual to determine right from wrong for himself.

In this libertarian environment, Christianity faces its greatest foe. The fires of persecution tend to strengthen the resolve of the saints, but a spirit of tolerance and permissiveness lowers the guard of believers and easily deceives them into embracing compromise.

So should it not surprise us, in this generation when lawlessness is abounding, to see the love of many growing cold? And yet God is too jealous to allow all of His saints to grow cold in their love. So what does He do? **He sends fiery affliction to His people in order turn their hearts back to Himself, and in order to seal their love.** The psalmist declared, "Before I was afflicted I went astray, but now I keep Your word" (Psalm 119:67). Just as the Israelites' affliction in Egypt caused them to cry out to God for a deliverer, even so our afflictions will put a deep cry within our hearts for our Deliverer, our heavenly Bridegroom, to come for us. Without that affliction, we become accustomed to Egypt and leave our first love.

To the one who allows affliction and crisis to kindle a deeper love the promise comes: "Because he has set his love upon Me, therefore I will deliver him; I will set him on high, because he has known My name" (Psalm 91:14).

25

THE LOVE HERMENEUTIC

The Scriptures are given to us for a very explicit reason: that we might love God with our entire being, and that we might love our neighbor as ourselves. Paul emphatically states that God gave us the Scriptures in order to perfect our love for Him and for one another: "Now the purpose of the commandment is love from a pure heart, from a good conscience, and from sincere faith" (1 Timothy 1:5).

In the verses previous (1 Timothy 1:1-4), Paul makes it clear that the Bible was not written to provoke philosophical debate nor to encourage the pursuit of theological bunnytrails.

The purpose of the Scriptures is love. The Bible has been given to us in order to incite and perfect our love. If my time in the Bible does not increase my love for God, I've missed the whole point. **Furthermore, if my teaching or preaching of God's word does not draw the listeners toward a more fervent love for Christ, then I have abused the Scriptures**.

Everything in the Bible must be seen as somehow directing our hearts more fully into the love of Christ. If there's a passage you don't understand, look at it by asking this question, "How does this passage point me toward the love of God?" You may be amazed at what you find. The only way you can understand any passage in the Bible is if you see it as somehow moving you toward the love of God.

I have discovered that some passages which have puzzled me have come clearer to me as I've looked at them through the lens of love. I call this "the love hermeneutic." The love hermeneutic analyzes and interprets a portion of Scripture through this question, "How can I see the love of God in these verses?"

To understand this love hermeneutic, come with me to some passages that have opened to me in new ways as I've considered how these verses direct my heart toward the love of God.

"Lest They Should Turn"

I've always been somewhat baffled by Jesus' response to His disciples when they asked Him why He always spoke to the crowds in parables:

> And He said to them, "To you it has been given to know the mystery of the kingdom of God; but to those who are outside, all things come in parables, so that 'Seeing they may see and not perceive, and hearing they may hear and not understand; lest they should turn, and their sins be forgiven them'" (Mark 4:11-12).

I could never understand why God would purposefully hide His truth from people, lest they should repent. The Bible says God wants men everywhere to repent — so why should God conceal His truth in such a way that men wouldn't repent?

To answer this question, let's employ "the love hermeneutic" and look at these words through the lens of love. God purposes that men everywhere love His Son, the Lord Jesus. Jesus presented the kingdom message in such a way that men had to make a personal decision regarding Him — whether to love Him or not.

God's concern was that men might hear the truth, be persuaded at an intellectual level to repent, and actually have their sins forgiven **but not have a love for Jesus Christ**. The message was veiled so that men would not repent simply on a rational level alone. God has purposed that repentance come at the heart/love level, not the cerebral/head level.

No Wedding Garment

Here's another passage that I haven't understood:

> "So those servants went out into the highways and gath-
> ered together all whom they found, both bad and good.
> And the wedding hall was filled with guests. But when
> the king came in to see the guests, he saw a man there
> who did not have on a wedding garment. So he said to
> him, 'Friend, how did you come in here without a wed-
> ding garment?' And he was speechless. Then the king
> said to the servants, 'Bind him hand and foot, take him
> away, and cast him into outer darkness; there will be weep-
> ing and gnashing of teeth'" (Matthew 22:10-13).

My question has been this: how could someone get into the
marriage supper of the Lamb without a wedding garment?

By viewing this passage through the lens of love, I believe we
come up with a satisfactory answer. Jesus is illustrating what it
might be like for someone to get to heaven on the basis of an intellectual decision of repentance rather than a love for Christ. Without having gained a love for the Lamb, such a person would not be
clothed properly in the garments of love.

When asked, "Friend, how did you come in here without a
wedding garment?", the man should have said, "All I know is, I
love You!" But He couldn't say that. He didn't love the King — he
was speechless. Since he didn't love, he was cast out of the kingdom.

These verses emphasize that there is only one way to become a
member of the Bride of Christ: you've got to love the Groom. The
big question becomes the question Jesus directed to Simon Peter:
"Do you love Me?"

A reader might complain to me, "Bob, you're stepping out into
realms of conjecture. You can't substantiate that the man without
the wedding garment didn't love Christ." You don't have to accept
my method of interpretation here, but I think I'm on to something.
Viewing these verses through the lens of love (1 Timothy 1:5) tips
us off to the fact that this man tried to enter the kingdom through a
route other than love.

Men can dissect the gospel rationally. They can weigh its pros and cons. But God has constructed the kingdom so that the only way men will respond to the gospel is in love. We are commissioned to show them the cross and then ask, "Will you love this Jesus?"

Why Was Andrew Excluded?

I have wondered why Jesus chose Peter, James and John as the three to enjoy some of the most outstanding experiences of Jesus' ministry. For example, those three were the only ones to see the most glorious highlight of Jesus' days on earth — I'm referring to Christ's transfiguration on the mountain. James and John were brothers, and Jesus included them both in the three. But Peter and Andrew were also brothers, and yet Jesus included Peter but excluded Andrew.

Why was Andrew excluded? The answer, I believe, is love. Jesus taught that to those who have, more will be given. Jesus knew which three loved Him the most, and because they loved they knew the greatest glory. Their diligence qualified them for this fantastic experience. James' love for Jesus is manifest in the fact that he was the first of the Twelve to be martyred (Acts 12:2). There must have been some kind of quiet dynamism and fervency in the heart of James, unrevealed to us, that incited the Jews to target him with their antagonism. James burned with a fiery love for Jesus and was killed for it. God doesn't show favoritism, but He has His favorites—He reserves the highest encounters for those who diligently seek Him, and walk in abandoned obedience.

Jesus said, "To him who has, more will be given." If you have love, He'll impart even more to you. I believe this is seen in Andrew's life. Andrew could have had his nose bent out of shape: "I brought my brother Simon Peter to Jesus in the first place, and now he's taken precedence over me!" He could have become bitter and offended, but instead he kept a guard on his heart and followed hard after Jesus. In the end, Andrew was rewarded for his diligence. At the end of His ministry, when Jesus opened up the future to His disciples and revealed to them the things that would take place in the last days, there were not three present but four! Jesus gave this revelation to Peter, James, John, **and Andrew** (Mark 13:3). Why is Andrew now included? Because he had given himself to love.

Parable Of The Talents

Finally, let's look at Jesus' parable of the talents through the lens of love, and specifically at the one who was given the one talent but buried it. Jesus told it like this:

> "Then he who had received the one talent came and said, 'Lord, I knew you to be a hard man, reaping where you have not sown, and gathering where you have not scattered seed. And I was afraid, and went and hid your talent in the ground. Look, there you have what is yours'" (Matthew 25:24-25).

Ultimately Jesus said of him, "Cast the unprofitable servant into the outer darkness" (Matthew 25:30). This man was excluded from the kingdom because he did not love. He feared, but he didn't love. His distorted view of the Master as being a hard man was evidence of the fact that he didn't truly know the Master.

This parable illustrates the truth that love is fruitful, but fear buries. Fear (represented in the one who buried his talent) will cause us to be unfruitful, but love (represented in the ones who cultivated their talents) will launch us into greater dimensions of kingdom productivity and blessing.

26

PERFECTED IN LOVE

The Scriptures testify that our God is a consuming fire. Paul wrote that God dwells in "unapproachable light" (1 Timothy 6:16). Wow! What a gripping description of God! God dwells in a light that's so bright that we can't bear to get close to it. This light is unapproachable because it's also a fire. It's a fiery inferno that emits an unapproachable light, and it's God's home.

God gave us fire so that we could understand Him better. He also gave us stars so we could better understand what He's doing in us — the natural order instructing us in the spiritual order. The Bible says we will shine like stars (Daniel 12:3; Matthew 13:43), and to understand that we need to appreciate what causes a star to burn.

The thing that causes a star to burn, in simple terms, is its gravity. The larger the mass, the greater the gravity. Stars have such a large mass that their gravity is enormous. When the particles within a star are compressed together that tightly (because of gravity), fusion happens. The atoms fuse together in a nuclear reaction, emitting tremendous amounts of light and heat. Thus, stars are like huge nuclear reactors.

Jesus said we'll be like the angels in heaven, and we'll shine forth like the sun. The word "glory" in the Bible literally means "heaviness" or "weightiness." In other words, God will bestow such weightiness of glory upon us that we will explode from within — almost like the nuclear reaction that occurs in the core of a star

— and we'll emit radiant beams of light from the very core of our being as we face the throne of God.

If we will shine like stars, and the angels shine like stars, how much more the God of the universe must shine! His glory (weightiness) is so incredible that there is a fusion-like eruption that eminates forth from His innermost being, which is an effusion of light and heat. It is the fire of His presence. This light and fire is unapproachable—at least to natural man.

Everlasting Fire

All of us will dwell with everlasting burning. The only question is, which fire will it be? The fire of God's love, or the fire of God's wrath? Both fires actually have the same source — God Himself.

In Matthew 13:41-43, Jesus testified that we are all destined for eternal fire. Every human will burn for eternity. Some will be thrown into the furnace of fire, and the others will burn as the sun in the kingdom of their Father. Even as God is a consuming fire, we will become blazing infernos of His love and holiness.

Fire becomes you, dear saint. Have salt in yourself, and have fire in yourself. Let the zeal of the Lord consume you. Be a flame that is ignited with the fire of God's love!

The Purpose Of Fiery Trials

In order for you and I to become aflame with the zeal of God's love, we must experience fiery trials. The very purpose of such trials is that we may be perfected in love.

> 1 John 4:17, "Love has been perfected among us in this: that we may have boldness in the day of judgment; because as He is, so are we in this world. 18 There is no fear in love; but perfect love casts out fear, because fear involves torment. But he who fears has not been made perfect in love."

When we don't fully understand God's purposes in fiery trials, our tendency is to fear. Some of my friends have looked at me and thought, "Oh no, if God did that to Bob, I wonder what He's going to do to me." We fear because we don't properly appreciate what God's fire produces within us. In all honesty, I have trembled before God's fire, thinking that if He could wound me like this, then He could wound me even more. Then as I've labelled that fear I've come to realize that I'm not yet perfected in love. **Love is perfected when God's servant no longer fears the fiery dealings of God, but fully embraces in His heart the great mercy that is touching his life.**

This perfected love is attained through months, even years, of the intense heat of God's furnace. The afflicted servant has no control over this process, but waits for the day when God reveals Himself to him. It is a glorious day when the saint can say from the midst of the fire with true abandonment, "Burn, fire, burn. Love of God, consume me. Let Your fire burn in my heart, Lord, until all is consumed but love." According to verse 17, when this love is perfected in the heart, there comes great boldness to appear before the throne of Christ. When you've persevered through God's fire in this life, you gain great boldness to face the fire of His judgment that will be applied to all our lives before His throne.

John's Reward

> I, John, both your brother and companion in the tribulation and kingdom and patience of Jesus Christ, was on the island that is called Patmos for the word of God and for the testimony of Jesus Christ. I was in the Spirit on the Lord's Day, and I heard behind me a loud voice, as of a trumpet (Revelation 1:9-10).

John was suffering under fiery persecution as an exile on a lonely island. He had done nothing deserving of imprisonment, but was suffering unjustly because of the word of God and the testimony of Jesus.

John had come to the place where he loved God in the midst of the fire. This is evidenced by his statement, "I was in the Spirit on the Lord's Day." He was lonely, rejected, treated unjustly, and separated from all ministry expression. He could have been having a pity party on the Lord's Day. But instead, how do we find John?

He's "in the Spirit"! He was loving Jesus in the midst of his pain. His heart was right in his sufferings, and he was honoring the Lord's Day.

In that place of right attitude and obedience, God came to him and gave him a mighty revelation of Christ (contained in the Book of Revelation). Lord, how I long for You to come to me and give me a revelation of Christ as well! If John had entertained a lousy attitude, he would have never had the revelation.

No doubt the enemy tried to come to John and say, "Look at you. You loved the Lord, you leaned on His breast, you were called the disciple whom Jesus loved — but look where all this love has gotten you. Here you are, rotting on this God-forsaken island. Where has your love for Jesus gotten you, anyway?"

Instead of grumbling and complaining, John got in the Spirit. His imprisonment proved that his love was perfected. He kept his heart right in the midst of the fire and was rewarded for it. If you will fasten your love upon the Lord in the midst of your suffering, He will reward you too.

A Love That's Better Than Life

David also understood the importance of keeping his heart right in the midst of undeserved distress. Look at what David wrote while in the wilderness of Judah: "Your lovingkindness is better than life" (Psalm 63:3). Saul was chasing him down, seeking to snuff out his life, but David was soaking in the love of God. David had two opportunities to kill Saul, but he refused. David was saying, "If Saul chases me down and kills me, I'd rather die while having this love of God filling my soul, than to take revenge on my enemy and lose God's affections."

We have a choice: the pursuit of fulfillment in this life or the pursuit of God's lovingkindness. His lovingkindness takes us the way of death. "Seek to find your life, and you'll lose it. Lose it, and you'll find it." When David chose God's love, he was choosing the wilderness.

David was saying, "I love being with You and enjoying Your love more than any other pursuit or pleasure in this life." You know love has been perfected in your heart when you would rather be in the arms of Jesus than do anything else. More than watching a movie, more than being with friends, more than enjoying a recreational activity, more than going on a cruise — more than anything — I'd rather spend time with You, Lord Jesus.

There is a love that is better than anything and everything else in this life. May the Lord perfect us in this love!

God's Deliverance

David didn't conduct himself perfectly in every single area of his life, but even in the midst of his mistakes there was a deep cry in his heart for God. David experienced Psalm 91:14 first-hand, where God testified: "Because he has set his love upon Me, therefore I will deliver him; I will set him on high, because he has known My name." Because he was chasing after God in his heart and loving God in the midst of his distresses, the Lord delivered him. Not only did God deliver him, He also honored him and promoted him.

I've decided that I can be wrong on a theological point, but if I'm loving Him I'm a winner. And the opposite is also true: I can be right theologically, but if I'm not loving Him I'm a loser. It really is the first and greatest commandment: Love the Lord your God.

When you are in distressing circumstances, I would encourage you to simply set your love upon God. Fasten your affections upon Him, and give Him your love no matter what may come your way. God destines a deliverance for those who will love Him in the midst of their trials and calamity. It is in this way that our love for the Lord is perfected. Perfected love sees the purposes of God in life's distresses. Not only does love gain a great deliverance, but it also purchases a maturity that has allowed the fiery circumstances to refine and perfect Christlike character.

Expressions Of Sincerity That Perfect Love

I'm a Martha (a doer) by nature. God is in the process of making me a lover first and a doer second, but this is requiring a major overhaul in the essence of my temperament. In my case, God is using a season of great personal crisis to bring me to a new level of worship relationship with Him. I am witnessing how masterfully the Lord allows unsettling circumstances to dislodge us from the smallness of our present experience, to bring us to greater depths of maturity and dependence upon Him.

I see three progressive levels of consecration in our personal worship lives: discipline, delight, and desperation. We all begin at the discipline level, establishing a worship relationship that is built upon commitment to a disciplined regimen of time spent with God. Eventually, the Lord brings us to the place where we long to spend time with Him because He has become our true delight. But I'm discovering an even higher worship dimension which I call "desperate dependence." At this level, the Lord allows crisis to drive us into His face. His smile becomes our only source of sanity. The Lord Jesus is pursued with the fervency of a drowning man. Every word from His mouth is like another gulp of air. Time spent with Him becomes a matter of sheer survival. It is this level of mature dependence that is so extravagantly depicted in the leaning bride of Song of Solomon 8:5.

The present impetus of the Spirit seems to be a call to intimacy with Jesus. Something within us cries out in response, "Lord, how can my relationship with you be more immediate and alive?" I've found the following thoughts helpful as I've pressed into the knowledge of Jesus Christ:

- I usually spend my "quiet time" with the Lord in the morning. But I've found it meaningful to stop a couple times during the course of a day, get on my face before God, and reaffirm that He is all I live for. This adds a certain sense of sincerity to my love for the Lord.
- When at a social event, quietly slip away from the crowd for a few minutes, and tell the Lord that you love Him even more than the warmth of human friendships. The response of the Lord Jesus to this kind of sincerity is really quite incredible.
- I remind myself that my time with Him is an end in itself, and not a means to an end. I used to subconsciously view my devotional life with Jesus as a necessary time of receiving if I wanted to have something to give out. But I began to see that my soul was being energized more by the reward of fruitful service than the joy of just knowing

Him. There is a certain intimacy that opens to us when we measure our personal significance by the degree to which we touch the heart of God in worship, instead of measuring it by ministry accomplishments.

- Take an occasional retreat of several days' duration, perhaps once a year. I'd like to commend three ingredients that have made retreats most significant for me: fasting, solitude, and an immersion in the Gospels. When you come alive by the power of the Holy Spirit to the Jesus of the Gospels, your worship life will be transformed.

27

A SIMPLE PRAYER

The Lord gave me a three-fold prayer earlier this year that I have used in my personal time with Him, and I have found it a great way to commence my intimacy with Him in the morning. It's very simple, but I think you'll enjoy incorporating this three-fold prayer into your personal devotional life:

Prayer #1: "Lord, I believe and receive Your love for me."

The Lord says to you, "'Yes, I have loved you **with an everlasting love**; therefore with lovingkindness I have drawn you'" (Jeremiah 31:3).

So respond to Him just now and say, "Lord, I believe that You love me. And now I receive Your love." We are not capable of loving Him until we have first received His love for us.

John wrote, "And we have known and believed the love that God has for us" (1 John 4:16). Many believers have yet to fully apprehend this verse. They still struggle with the thought that God could love them. "Love **me**?" they ask. "How could God love a mess like **me**?"

Dearly beloved of God, this must be settled once for all in your spirit. You must realize that God loves you personally and passionately, not because of who you are but because of who He is. God's love for you is not based upon who you are or what you've done but upon who He is and what He's done (in Calvary). His heart is so great that He reaches out to all mankind with the true heart of a Father.

Hear the Father's heart in John 3:16, "For God **so loved the world** that He gave His only begotten Son, that whoever believes in Him should not perish but have **everlasting life.**" The word "everlasting" denotes both **quantity** and **quality**. God's life is everlasting in **quantity**: God's life is so full and replete that it will last for eternity. And God's life is everlasting in **quality**: God's life is so dynamically vibrant that nothing can kill it, not even eternity itself. God says, "I'm going to pour a quality of life into you that is unlike any kind of life you've ever known. This life is so incredibly dynamic and abundant that I call it everlasting life." It is a life that emanates from the eternal lifesource of God Himself.

God uses the same adjective to describe His love for us. He says He loves us "with an everlasting love" (Jeremiah 31:3) Again, the word "everlasting" denotes both **quantity** and **quality**. God's love is everlasting in **quantity** — that is, He is so full of love for us that the storehouse of His love will never run dry. For all eternity, the flame of His love will never flicker and die because it is fed from an eternal source. But even more significantly, God's love is everlasting in **quality** — that is, the fire of His love for us is so rich and full and deep that nothing can snuff it out. One source defines the New Testament word for love — "agape" — as "unconquerable benevolence and undefeatable goodwill." This love of God is described as "everlasting," not simply because it will last for ever and ever, but because of the **kind** of love it is. It is a love that blazes with such fiery intensity that it cannot be extinguished by anything — not even by eternity. Long after eternity has quenched the fire of our sun, God's love will continue to burn with the same passion He displayed for you during His crucifixion.

Stop just now and say it again, "Lord, I receive Your incredible love for me."

Prayer #2: "Lord, I love You."

Make this the second statement in your personal prayer time. It's good to **tell Him** you love Him.

Find ways to amplify upon that. Search your heart for words to express your innermost feelings and thoughts. Learn to become increasingly expressive in your passions for Him. Ask the Holy Spirit to help you because it takes God to love God.

Fear and love move along the same channel in our hearts. There is a river that flows from our hearts to God, and Jesus said in John 7:38 that this river of love is energized by the Holy Spirit. But Satan wants to hinder the flow by causing us to fear. **Fear is the "backwash" that runs countercurrent to God's love, and it seeks to impede, repress, and immobilize our love for God.** 1 John 4:18 assures us, however, that "perfect love casts out fear."

The Lord wants us to be flooded with such a rushing flow of the Holy Spirit that fear is literally flushed from our lives on the current of His love.

"Lord, I want to be perfected in this love. I really do love You!"

David prayed, "O God, my heart is steadfast" (Ps. 108:1). David was saying, "My heart isn't wavering, O God. I'm not up and down, hot and cold. Rather, I'm constant in my fervency for You." God's love is said to be steadfast (Lamentations 3), and now David says he has the same kind of love for God. In one word, this love is called "constancy."

David is saying, "The fervency of my love for You is constant. I continually press into Your face with unabated passion. I have the same kind of love for You that You have for me."

Take time every day to tell Him you love Him. And tell Him your fervency for Him burns as brightly today as it ever has.

Prayer #3: "Lord, how can I love my neighbor today?"

Jesus said, "This is My commandment, that you love one another as I have loved you" (John 15:12).

Henri Nouwen has said, "It's an incredible mystery of God's love that the more you know how deeply you are loved, the more you will see how deeply your sisters and your brothers in the human family are loved."

When I fully come to love God perfectly and to share His heart, I will find myself effortlessly loving those whom He loves.

There is only one thing to live for, and that is the affirmation of Jesus. How does one receive the King's nod? One of the greatest secrets of touching His heart is to touch the people He loves so passionately.

Here's some simple "kingdom math":

$$\text{ministry} - \text{love} = \text{burnout}$$
$$\text{ministry} + \text{love} = \text{fruitfulness}$$

To explain, if my service to others is not motivated by love for Christ, I am facing inevitable burnout. But if my ministry is the expression of my passionate love for Jesus, I will participate in genuine kingdom fruitfulness.

"Lord, may my love for others become the natural extension of my love for You. Teach me to love in such a way that I am carried along upon the impetus of Your incredible love for the world."

28

THE ULTIMATE PINNACLE

I want to finish this book by pointing to the zenith of all revealed truth. I have referred to the eighth chapter of Romans as "the Himalayas of the Bible" because no other single chapter in the entire Bible (in my opinion) has more pinnacles of glorious truth. Romans 8 is a veritable mountain range of some of the most sublime and inspiring truths in all of Scripture. And it culminates with the highest peak — the Mount Everest — of sacred revelation.

We leave the foothills behind and step out onto the first great peak of the Himalayas with Romans 8:1, "There is therefore now no condemnation to those who are in Christ Jesus, who do not walk according to the flesh, but according to the Spirit." There is a place in God where we live free from the enemy's accusations, and although it is a mighty mountain to climb, it is an attainable height in the grace of God. This is the first real mountain a Christian must climb. We could deal extensively with this tremendous mountain of truth, but I want to move quickly toward the greatest height.

The next great pinnacle in this chapter is Romans 8:11, "But if the Spirit of Him who raised Jesus from the dead dwells in you, He who raised Christ from the dead will also give life to your mortal bodies through His Spirit who dwells in you."

From there we go to the tremendous heights of Romans 8:15, "For you did not receive the spirit of bondage again to fear, but you received the Spirit of adoption by whom we cry out, 'Abba, Father.'" "Abba" is the Aramaic word for Father that Jesus actually spoke in everyday language, and when we use that same word we sound just like Jesus and touch the heart of the Father in a remarkable way.

Dealing With Suffering

The next three pinnacles of Romans 8 all give us mountaintop perspectives on how to deal with suffering as a Christian.

- "For I consider that the sufferings of this present time are not worthy to be compared with the glory which shall be revealed in us" (Romans 8:18). (Paul indicates that the ratio of suffering to eternal glory is disproportionate — that is, that a **little** suffering here turns into **great** glory there. No suffering, no glory. The greater the suffering, the greater the glory.)

- "Likewise the Spirit also helps in our weaknesses. For we do not know what we should pray for as we ought, but the Spirit Himself makes intercession for us with groanings which cannot be uttered" (Romans 8:26). (This verse says that when we're in pain, the Spirit helps us pray. He helps us travail, in intercession, unto the birthing of God's purposes in our lives.)

- "And we know that all things work together for good to those who love God, to those who are the called according to His purpose" (Romans 8:28).

I've got to slow down and take some time with Romans 8:28. As we progress through the pinnacles of Romans 8, verse 28 stands out as one of the most awesome truths of all Scripture. The assurance of this verse is simply this: God works painful circumstances together for good — if we'll just love Him in the midst of our distress.

This truth is illustrated beautifully in the life of a certain woman in the Bible whose husband died seven years into their marriage. (Perhaps you'll guess to whom I'm referring.) The Bible gives no indication that she had any children. After her husband died, nobody else wanted to marry her. I suppose she would have loved to re-marry and have children, but no suitors came along.

It would have been tempting for her to become a bitter and lonely person. Life was extremely difficult for widows back in those times. I'm sure she got angry at God, at least in the early days. But instead of holding to her questions and anger and bitter-ness, she gave herself to loving God. In the midst of her personal heartache, she just loved God.

Slowly God's purposes began to unfold in her life, and she accepted the calling of a prophetess. The months turned into years, and the Bible says she "served God with fastings and prayers night and day." Her prayer most certainly would have been, "Lord, bring redemption to Israel!" By now you may have guessed that I'm referring to Anna. (See Luke 2:36-38.)

I believe Anna played a critical role of intercession in prepar-ing the way for the Messiah to be born in her day. She "prayed Him in" and then was given the joy of seeing Him herself.

God couldn't find a widow in Israel in the time of Elijah when He wanted to visit the nation. Jesus said there were many widows in Israel in the time of Elijah, but to none of them was Elijah sent. Elijah had to be sent to the home of a Gentile widow because there was no widow in Israel that He could trust. In Anna's day God wanted to visit the nation again, and just like in the days of Elijah, He looked for a widow in Israel who would be available for His purposes. This time, however, He didn't have to go outside the nation. God needed a widow who would not be distracted with other valid pursuits, but would be able to devote herself fully to her God-ordained task of intercession. In His sovereignty, He prepared Anna to be that widow. When He took her husband from her, I believe God was asking, "Anna, will you be that widow? Will you be the widow I need in this hour to prepare the way of the Messiah through intercession?" By just loving God through her pain, Anna qualified as the candidate for this sacred role.

When Joseph and Mary presented the infant Jesus to the Lord in the temple, Anna got to see the answer to her prayers. The Scrip-tures say it this way: "And coming in that instant she gave thanks to the Lord, and spoke of Him to all those who looked for redemption in Jerusalem" (Luke 2:38). What great honor she knew in the end! She got to behold and praise the Hope of Israel! Anna's life illustrates the truth of Romans 8:28: **the key to turning tragedy into triumph is by loving God through it all.**

Mount Everest

The last and greatest pinnacle of Romans 8 is what I would call the Mount Everest of the Bible. It represents the highest summit of biblical truth in the grace of God. I recall flying into Seattle one time, and during our approach we flew right past Mount Ranier. As I looked out the window, Mount Ranier filled the horizon and loomed far above our airplane as it jutted up into the sky.

Now, we're going to take a quick "flight" past Mount Everest. Turn and behold, and envision this immense mountain before you. This mountain is called "the love of God." **The love of God is the most magnificent and lofty of all scriptural truths.** It is the Mount Everest of the Bible. As you behold this mountain of God's love, you gasp in wonder as you declare, ""Behold what manner of love the Father has bestowed on us, that we should be called children of God!" (1 John 3:1). Paul said there are other pinnacles in the grace of God, such as faith and hope, "but the greatest of these is love" (1 Corinthians 13:13).

I want you to see the love of God as an immense mountain. Paul talks about the towering proportions of this vast mountain of God's love in Ephesians 3:18.

> Ephesians 3:17, That Christ may dwell in your hearts through faith; that you, being rooted and grounded in love, 18 may be able to comprehend with all the saints what is the width and length and depth and height— 19 to know the love of Christ which passes knowledge; that you may be filled with all the fullness of God.

"That you...may be able to comprehend with all the saints." As Paul calls us to delve deeper into God's love, he indicates that we will never uncover the love of God in a vacuum by ourselves. We'll only come to comprehend His love as we function in the corporate body of Christ. The fullness of God's love can be discovered only through the great diversity of the body of Christ. Our brothers and sisters will help us see and understand God's love.

"To know the love of Christ which passes knowledge." Based on that statement, I used to think God's love was beyond our grasp. But now I'm seeing this verse to mean that we won't grasp all of God's love with our **mind**; there are aspects to His love that we must **experience**. There are aspects to God's love that can be grasped only with the heart.

"That you may be filled with all the fullness of God." The key to unlocking the very fullness of God is to pursue God's love in all its dimensions.

The Dimensions Of God's Love

Ephesians 3:18	John 3:16	Description
"width"	"For God so loved the world"	God embraces people of every race, every social strata, every personality, and every evil extreme.
"length"	"that He gave His only begotten Son"	The cross represents the great lengths to which God went to reach from the heights of His holiness to touch man in the depths of his depravity.
"depth"	"that whoever believes in Him should not perish"	The interior of this cavernous mountain is a rich mine of infinite wealth which we will explore and uncover for all eternity.
"height"	"but have everlasting life"	This describes the glorious heights to which His love has lifted us.

This diagram points to the vast dimensions of this awesome and mighty mountain called the love of God. Like Mount Everest, it extends in four glorious dimensions:

Width: The mountain of God's love is so wide that its width is beyond measurement. God's arms stretch out so wide that no one is excluded from the grasp of His love. No sinner has gone to such extremes as to place himself outside the sweep of God's loving arms. God's love is wide enough to embrace every single human being across the entire expanse of our globe.

Length: This points to the downward limits of God's love. God's love is a mountain whose base reaches down to the depths of man's depravity. At the foot of this mountain — Mount Calvary — hangs a Man who humbled Himself to the point of dying on a cross. As we behold the cross, we see with unfolding clarity the awesome lengths of God's love that sent Christ from the glories of heaven to the abyss of man's sinfulness.

Depth: This refers to the interior dimension of the mountain of God's love. There are precious jewels of truth to be mined within this mountain, but they require diligent digging. Eternity will be a never-ending discovery of ever-unfolding revelation into the wonder and beauty and glory of God's unsearchable love.

Height: Finally, this Mount Everest of God's love thrusts upward into the sky before us, an awesome snow-capped pinnacle of incredible wonder. Behold the glorious heights to which God's love has lifted us! When His love tells us that we've been made to sit with Christ in heavenly places, we can only gape at such revelation with wonder and amazement. Our hearts soar upon the winds that sweep across the jutting summit of God's expansive love.

Nothing Shall Separate Us

As a reminder we've been looking at the pinnacle truths of Romans 8. Now, as we come to the end of this great chapter, we face the highest pinnacle of all, the Mount Everest of the Bible:

> Romans 8:35, Who shall separate us from the love of Christ? Shall tribulation, or distress, or persecution, or famine, or nakedness, or peril, or sword? 36 As it is writ-

ten: "For Your sake we are killed all day long; we are
accounted as sheep for the slaughter." 37 Yet in all these
things we are more than conquerors through Him who
loved us. 38 For I am persuaded that neither death nor
life, nor angels nor principalities nor powers, nor things
present nor things to come, 39 nor height nor depth, nor
any other created thing, shall be able to separate us from
the love of God which is in Christ Jesus our Lord.

In this passage, Paul is exploring the marvelous truth that nothing shall separate us from the love of God which is in Christ. Patricia Blue has said, "Sin separates us from His presence, but nothing separates us from His love."

Unconditional Love
As I meditated in this passage, I began to wonder if my kids could do anything to cut off my love from their lives. I have three children whom I love desperately — Joel, Katie, and Michael — and I can't think of anything that would cause me to stop loving them.

I was able to imagine some possible scenarios in which my children could potentially make me absolutely furious; I was able to imagine some possible scenarios in which my children could hurt and wound me terribly; but I could not imagine a single scenario in which my children could do something that would cause me to remove my love from them.

So if I, being evil, love my children with that kind of unconditional tenacity, **how much more** will God, who says He loves us with an everlasting love, never remove His love from us! Nothing can ever separate us from His love because **we're His kids**. No matter what you do, or no matter what happens to you, He still loves you.

Verse 36 goes on to say, "As it is written: 'For Your sake we are killed all day long; we are accounted as sheep for the slaughter.'" In this verse Paul describes New Testament Christianity. We thought the full expression of what it really means to be a Christian was, "Power, might, dominion, and strength!" We thought the fully matured New Testament Christian caught bullets with his teeth and leapt over tall buildings with a single bound. But what Paul describes in this verse sounds more like being conformed to Christ's death. **The true image of Christian maturity is that of a sheep being slaughtered.**

"Yet in all these things we are more than conquerors through Him who loved us" (Romans 8:37). Notice that Paul says, "in all these things." In all what things? In all the things of verse 35: tribulation, distress (pain), persecution, famine, nakedness (poverty), peril (violence), and sword (war). Paul affirms that New Testament Christians experience verse 35 and look like verse 36!

More Than Conquerors

"Yet in all these things we are more than conquerors." When I picture a conqueror in my mind, I envision someone such as a boxing champion. His arms are raised; his face is proud; his muscles are rippling; he's prancing about in a victory dance; he's strong; he has an air of invincibility about him; he's undefeated — he's the champion! But Paul doesn't paint that picture of the Christian. Instead, the image he uses is that of a sheep going to slaughter. Now, a sheep going to slaughter doesn't look anything like what I thought a conqueror resembles.

Sometimes I've thought, "Lord, I don't even look like a **conqueror**, never mind **more** than a conqueror!" So I've sought to know what Paul meant by that term, "more than conquerors."

I hear Paul saying, "We're more than conquerors because we've got Christ's love." We're weak, broken, and hurting — but we've got Christ's love. So even when it looks like we're losing, the fact that we have this awesome love means we're winning. With a love like this, who can lose? If losing my life means I get to have this love, then to lose is to gain.

Paul is inferring, "The worse I look, the greater my victory." The world says, "That's not conquering." No, it's **more** than conquering. It's winning in the midst of weakness.

"In fact," I can hear Paul continuing, "if you kill me, then I've just won the highest victory!" Martyrdom truly is the noblest of victories.

More than conquerors means this: the feeblest army pulls off the greatest victory.

Based on Romans 8, here's my present understanding of how the kingdom works: God's saints are harassed, persecuted, and pained in many ways as they press with great zeal and suffering into the fullness of God's purposes. God allows Satan to hinder them, and they suffer many setbacks and much perplexity. But God is faithful, and He delivers them out of all their troubles when they keep their heart right before Him. In this way, the forces of hell are conquered by a weak and dependent church. This church does not conquer by God using His overriding power to sovereignly blast through every obstacle as soon as it surfaces. Instead, they persevere through calamity and pain and crisis, but in the end they have a testimony of the unfailing grace of God, and Satan is defeated by the most pitiful army you've ever seen. God in His grace has upended His rival with broken, wounded, faithful lovers of Jesus Christ. In the process of the pain they are perfected into the image of Christ, and Satan has no accusation against the justice of God, for God has not blown Satan out of the water just by virtue of His power. Rather, in His wisdom, God has chosen the weak things of this world to confound the might of Satan. **In the end, Satan will be furious at being defeated by such an ignoble army, and God will be glorified at the greatness of His grace which was able to effect such a victory through such limited means.**

God's Response

When you're living in the pressure, pain, persecution, and neediness of verse 35, you don't **feel** like a conqueror. You feel more like hamburger. You're loving Him, but you **feel** terrible. You feel like you're **dying**.

But something powerful happens at this point. As God looks down upon this suffering servant, He sees a saint that is not opening his mouth. He's not complaining; he's not angry at God. He's submitting meekly to the sufferings of Christ. And he's just loving God.

As God beholds this suffering saint He says, "He...he looks like My Son! That's exactly how My Son died! This saint reminds

Me of My Son, the resemblance is incredible!" And something of
the infinite love of God is unlocked from within the Father's heart.
This kind of sacrifice touches the Father and literally melts His
heart. **When you look like a slaughtered lamb, in the Father's
eyes you look just like Jesus.** You can't imagine what happens
when you begin to crack open the eternal storehouses of God's
love in this way.

Here's the saint — hurting, distressed, bruised — and he's getting blitzed with the Father's love! Paul is saying, "When this kind
of love is being poured on me, it doesn't matter how much pain I'm
in, I can't lose!"

Paul learned that first-hand ever before he was a Christian.
While still named Saul, he watched while Stephen was stoned to
death. As the stones were pummeling his body, Stephen wasn't
saying, "Ouch! Oooh! Augh! Oh that hurts!" Instead, Stephen
was saying, "Look! I see the heavens opened and the Son of Man
standing at the right hand of God!" (Acts 7:56). Jesus, who is seated
at the right hand of God in heaven, actually stood up to greet this
first martyr of our faith.

Stephen can hardly even feel the rocks because the heavens
have opened before him, and Jesus is pouring upon him an affection like he's never known. His body is being stoned to death, but
his soul is being baptized in love. I can imagine Stephen thinking,
"Don't stop now, guys, go all the way. Do a good job of it! I see my
Beloved, and my heart yearns to be with Him."

Oh, when the Father pours this love on you! In verse 28 Paul
talks about what happens **when we love God** (and that's great).
But here in verse 37 he talks about something far more glorious —
what happens **when God loves us!**

The assurance of verses 37-38 is this: When you're laying your
life down as a sheep for the slaughter, there is nothing that can
hinder this love of God from pouring all over you! **Tribulation
and distress are the very portals that open up the highest dimensions of God's love!**

O the weakness of my ability to show you this mountain of
God's love! Look away once again at the summit of this glorious
mountain, the Mount Everest of the grace of God:

"For I am persuaded that neither death nor life, nor angels nor principalities nor powers, nor things present nor things to come, nor height nor depth, nor any other created thing, shall be able to separate us from the love of God which is in Christ Jesus our Lord" (Romans 8:38-39).

Hallelujah!

From Your Grace Flows

Words and Music:
Bob Sorge

(From Your Grace Flows, page 2)